Table of Contents

Table of Contents

Table of Contents

Table of Contents

Table of Contents

Table of Contents

Introduction

Hi, my name is Elsie Yan and I live in Kuala Lumpur, Malaysia. I am in my early sixties and have been living low carb for over 6 years now. Living low carb has helped me lose some weight and get healthier.

As I love to cook, I experimented with low carb / keto recipes and shared them on my social medias. Eventually, I started my youtube channel "lowcarbrecipeideas" 4 years ago and have published close to 400 videos as of today.

I launched my first e-book in August this year titled "The Ultimate Keto Bread Recipes". This e-book contains a total of 73 recipes with 61 non-vegan, 12 vegan recipes, important tips and tutorial as well. I am glad that it has been well received so far.

Introduction

Then I started working on my second e-book on "The Ultimate Low Carb / Keto Cake Recipes" as I have close to 100 recipes since I started my youtube channel. Cake is one of the easiest foods to be made low carb or keto. So yes,, you can have your cake and eat it too!

I like to use coconut flour in most of my cake recipes as it is way cheaper and healthier too. I have also used ground sunflower seeds, black and white sesame seeds in certain cake recipes. However, in most of my cake recipes, I have provided options for both almond, coconut flours and a combo of both flours so you can choose your preference. And I have also provided dairy free options whenever I can.

All my recipes are free of grains, gluten, wheat and sugar. My principle is to make them as easy as possible with no tools required unless absolutely necessary, so we have less cleaning to do.

Today, I am sharing all of my keto cake recipes in this book for your convenience. The videos for all these recipes are available in my youtube channel. I hope you find this book useful and thank you for your support!

IMPORTANT TIPS & TUTORIAL

PLEASE READ THESE IMPORTANT TIPS & TUTORIAL BEFORE MAKING ANY RECIPE FROM THIS E-BOOK

1. <u>TYPE OF FLOUR</u>

(a) <u>Almond Flour</u>

The most commonly used low carb flour for cakes. It has a more neutral color and taste with a heavier and denser texture. Almond flour has a 1:1 ratio with most regular flours. Though almond flour is easily available in most countries, but it is quite costly.

(b) <u>Coconut Flour</u>

Coconut flour is super absorbent hence, more eggs and liquid are required. It is very suitable for cakes as it produces a much lighter texture and, in most recipes, the coconut flavor is not obvious as it is masked by other flavors of the cake. It is way cheaper and healthier too. For cakes, we need to use the super fine coconut flour, not the coarse type as they are unable to absorb the liquid. Some coconut flours are more absorbent than others so you may find the batter to be thicker. In such cases, you may need to add more liquid. I suggest you try other brands and once you get the correct type, just stick to it. Coconut flour is not 1:1 ratio with other flour due to its high absorbency hence only a small amount is required. To replace almond flour, only 25% of coconut flour is required. Hence, for 120 g of almond flour, use only 30 g of coconut flour.

1. <u>TYPE OF FLOUR</u>

(c) <u>Sunflower Seeds</u>

Ground sunflower seeds are a great alternative for low carb flour as they are way cheaper and healthier too. I have used it a lot in my keto bread recipes and it produces the best rise and texture. I have also tried it in keto cakes and even though the texture is a little denser and heavier, it is a great alternative especially if you are looking for a nut free option. Due to its high fat content, it can make the cake quite moist hence, we need to reduce the amount of liquid. The downside is that the sunflower seed flavor is quite strong, so I try to use it for stronger flavored cakes like chocolate, coffee, pumpkin pie spice etc. so the flavor is masked. Ground sunflower seeds have a 1:1 ratio with almond flour except that we need to reduce the amount of liquid such as the whipping cream by 20% while other ingredients remain the same.

(d) <u>Walnuts</u>

Raw walnuts are another great alternative for nut flours. I have used ground raw walnuts in making carrot, chocolate, coffee cakes and they turned out great. The texture is lighter than almond flour, but it has a darker color and is stronger in flavor hence, I limit it for stronger flavored cakes where color is not a concern too.

(e) <u>Black & White Sesame Seeds</u>

Ground black and white sesame seeds can be a good alternative for low carb flour as its cheap and healthy. However, its flavor is too strong, and it can produce a bitter taste when baked at high temperature for a certain period. Hence, I only used it to make black and white sesame cakes.

4

2. GRINDING OF NUTS & SEEDS

(a) I used super fine almond and coconut flour for all the cake recipes here. I can easily purchase them online or from baking ingredient shops.

(b) For raw sunflower, black and white sesame seeds and walnuts, I grind them at home using a multi grinder. You can also use a coffee / spice grinder or a powerful food processor. Multi grinders are the best as you can grind in bulk and store them in the fridge or freezer. They are also much more effective.

(c) Home grinding will not produce a super fine texture as the fat content of the nuts and seeds are still intact. Commercial grinding can be super fine as the fats are squeezed out and sold separately as oil and the leftover "cake" is ground into a fine powder which is sold separately as flour.

(d) All type of seeds can be ground by themselves. However, certain nuts such as walnuts and pecans need to be combined with coconut flour due to their high fat content. Coconut flour helps to absorb the excess fats and ease with the grinding process.

(e) It is fine if there are still some chunks as they add to the crunch. Do not over grind as it will turn into a paste or butter. Always pulse for a few seconds for a few times to avoid over grinding.

(f) I grind all my nuts, seeds, psyllium husks in bulk and store them in the fridge or freezer for convenience.

3. SUBSTITUTIONS

(a) I have provided options in most of my cake recipes where you can either use coconut flour, almond flour or a combo of almond and coconut flour. If the option is not stated in certain recipes, you can just calculate the ratio yourself. For e.g., if almond flour is 120 g, then coconut flour should be 25% of 120 g so it should be 30 g only. If you wish to combine both flours for e.g. almond flour is 240 g so you can use 120 g almond flour and 30 g coconut flour.

5

3. <u>SUBSTITUTIONS</u>

(b) I normally use whipping cream, but you can replace with sour cream or yogurt. For dairy free option, you can replace it with coconut cream or milk (with thick consistency). All at the same ratio.

(c) You can also replace the whipping cream with unsweetened pea, almond or any keto friendly milk. However, because of the difference in consistency, you need to reduce the amount by 15% and increase the fat (i.e. the butter or oil) by 70%.

(d) You can replace melted butter with coconut oil, olive oil or any keto friendly oil for a dairy free option.

4. <u>SWEETENER</u>

(a) I use Monkfruit for all my cake recipes, but you can use any other keto friendly sweetener.

(b) For recipes that require chilling such as cheesecake or frosting cream, I use Allulose as it will not taste grainy when chilled. However, if you do not mind the grainy taste then you can use any keto friendly sweetener. For baking however, I would not recommend Allulose as it browns too quickly so the cake will look super dark especially the crust.

(c) All my cake recipes taste mild to moderately sweet so you can adjust according to your preference.

5. <u>EGG WHITES</u>

You can use egg whites to replace whole eggs. The amount of egg whites should be doubled the number of whole eggs. The batter is a bit dry but will bake up fine. Even though the texture is slightly drierand the cake looks whiter, but it still tastes good. It's a great alternative for those who have problem with egg yolks.

6. <u>STORAGE OF CAKES</u>

(a) Cheesecakes and cakes with cream frosting needs to be refrigerated for up to a week. For freezing, it's best to freeze the cake without the cream frosting.

(b) Most of the cakes without frosting can be kept at room temperature for a few days provided you have a cool and dry climate. Otherwise, it's best to refrigerate earlier for up to a week and freeze for up to 3 months.

(c) Chilled or frozen cakes can be brought to room temperature by leaving them on the countertop or microwave for 30 to 40 seconds.

7. <u>TEMPERATURE OF INGREDIENTS</u>

Unless called for, all ingredients should be at room temperature so that the cake will bake up evenly in the oven.

8. <u>WEIGHING OF INGREDIENTS</u>

For best results, weigh all the ingredients for accuracy.

9. <u>PREVENT CRACKS & OVER-BROWNING</u>

To prevent cracks and over-browning,

(a) Bake at lower racks.

(b) Bake at lower temperature

(c) Use bigger pans so that the cake is shallower and cooks faster.

Banana Cake

Ingredients

DRY INGREDIENTS
Ground Sunflower Seed = 240 g / 2 cups
Other Low Carb Flour Options:
1. Almond Flour = 240 g / 2 cups
2. Coconut Flour = 60 g / 1/2 cup
(Important Note: For these 2 flour options, the amount of whipping cream should be 160 ml or ⅔ cup. The rest of the ingredients remains the same.)
Baking Powder = 8 g / 2 tsp
Baking Soda = 1/4 tsp (Optional)
Monk fruit = 80 g / 6 tbsp
Salt = 1/2 tsp
Cinnamon Powder = 1 to 2 tsp

WET INGREDIENTS

Eggs = 3 large (170 g)

Unsalted Melted Butter = 45 ml / 3 tbsp

Whipping Cream = 120 ml / 1/2 cup

Banana Extract = 2 to 4 tsp

(Note: I used Banana Extract from McCormick but you can use any good quality ones. If you are not counting carbs, you could add mashed bananas but just make sure that you reduce the amount of liquid accordingly to prevent too much moisture)

FOR TOPPING

1 large banana (optional) - sliced into half lengthwise

DIRECTIONS

1. Preheat the oven at 350F or 180C.

2. In a bowl, add all the dry ingredients and mix until well combined.

3, Add all the wet ingredients and mix until well combined. The batter should be thick and smooth.

4. Grease and line parchment paper on an 8x4 inch (20x10 cm) loaf pan

5. Pour batter into the pan and top with sliced bananas. This is optional but it really adds a nice touch.

6. Bake at the middle rack for about 30 to 40 minutes or until a wooden skewer comes out clean.

Total Servings = 13

Nutrition info per serving

Total Carb = 4.9 g Dietary Fiber = 0.9 g Net Carb = 3.1 g

Calories = 108 Total Fat = 9.3 g Protein = 2.7 g

Banana Walnut Muffins with real bananas
(With Eggless Option)

DRY INGREDIENTS
Coconut flour = 60 g / 1/2 cup
(OR Almond flour = 240 g / 2 cups)
Baking Powder = 8 g / 2 tsp
Baking Soda = 2 g / 1/2 tsp (Optional)
Salt = 2 g / 1/2 tsp
Cinnamon Powder = 1 tsp

WET INGREDIENTS
Ripe Medium Bananas = 2 / 150 g
Monk fruit= 30 g / 2 1/3 tbsp
Unsalted Melted Butter (room temp) = 60 ml / 1/4 cup
Whole Eggs = 2 large (115 g)
(OR 2 flax / chia eggs. Combine 14 g ground flaxseed or chia seeds
with 90 ml water. Stir to mix and let it sit for 10 to 15 minutes
until thickened)
Unsweetened Greek Yogurt = 80 g / 1/3 cup
Vanilla Extract = 1 tsp

Chopped Roasted Walnuts = 50 g / 1/2 cup

DIRECTIONS

1. Preheat the oven at 340F or 170C.

2. For eggless versions, prepare the flax eggs in advance to let it sit for about 10 to 15 minutes until thickened.

3. Mash the bananas. You can either mash them until chunky or fine. If the bananas are still firm, just microwave for about 60 seconds until softened. If the bananas are under ripe, you can bake them in the oven until the skin turns black and they will be ripe enough for usage.

4. In a bowl, add all the wet ingredients, whisk to combine then set aside.

5. In another bowl, add all the dry ingredients and mix to combine.

6. Add the wet into the dry ingredients and use a spatula to mix until combined. The batter is thick. The batter for the eggless version is thicker which is normal. The baked muffins for the eggless version are also denser but equally delicious.

7. Add the chopped roasted walnuts but reserve a small amount for topping.

8. Scoop the batter into the prepared paper cups. I used small and firm paper cups so each muffin is about 50 g and I got 10 servings.

9. Top with reserved chopped walnuts. Gently press down the walnuts so that they will stick to the batter during baking.

10. Bake for about 15 to 20 minutes or until cooked.

Total Servings = 10

Nutrition info per serving
Total Carb = 9.8 g Dietary Fiber = 2.9 g Net Carb = 6.9
g Calories = 214 Total Fat = 17 g Protein = 6.6 g

Basque Burnt Cheesecake (Original)

Ingredients

Cream Cheese (room temperature) = 400 g / 1 2/3 cups
(Note: I used Philadelphia Cream Cheese. It's best to use good quality cream cheese as it is after all, the star of the cake.)
Whole Eggs (room temperature) = 2 large (115 g)
Whipping or Heavy Cream (room temperature) = 220 ml / 1cup
Powdered Allulose = 80 g / 5 1/2 tbsp
Salt = 1 g
Vanilla extract = 1 tsp

DIRECTIONS

1.Preheat the oven at 428 F or 200 C. It's best to preheat the oven longer around 20 to 30 minutes so that it is hot enough. The burnt texture is created by the high temperature and shorter baking time.
2.I used a 6 inch or 15 cm round pan with 3" height. If you use a bigger pan, you need to increase the recipe. Roughly line with parchment paper and cut off any excess then set aside. If your pan is lower, then you may need to make the parchment paper higher to withstand the rise.

DIRECTIONS

3. It's important to bring the cream cheese, eggs and whipping cream to room temperature so that they blend together easily creating a smoother batter.

4. In a small bowl, lightly beat the eggs, salt and vanilla extract then set aside.

5. In a bigger bowl, add the cream cheese and use a spatula to mix until smooth.

6. Add the sweetener and mix until smooth and creamy.

7. Add half the egg mixture and whisk until combined.

8. Add the balance of the egg mixture and whisk until well combined.

9. Add the whipping cream and whisk until smooth and creamy.

10. Strain the batter into the pan to prevent any lumps.

11. Bake at the middle rack with top, bottom heat and fan for about 20 to30 mins. If you only have a conventional oven with regular bake option, then bring the rack higher as heat rises so the upper oven will be hotter. However, if your oven is top heating, make sure that the parchment paper is not touching the heating element to prevent any burning. As all ovens are different, pay attention to the darkening of the top. Rotate the pan midway to ensure even browning. If the top is not darkening fast enough, you may have to give up on the color as you can't keep on baking. Sometimes, you may have to reduce the temperature if the top is burning too fast. So, you need to adapt to the situation as every oven is different.

12. Once the top is dark enough, immediately remove the pan. If you wish to have a darker top, just switch to the top heat for a little while before removing the pan. After removing the pan, just give it a jiggle and if the cake is wobbly, then it is done. The texture will firm up as it cools.

13. Do not over bake the cake after 30 mins even if the top is not dark enough as the texture of the cake will be affected.

DIRECTIONS

14. During baking, the cake will rise but will sink down after some time.

15. Whether you prefer a creamy texture or a creamy texture with an oozy raw center or a firmer texture like regular cheesecake, it basically boils down to the baking time. For a creamy texture, bake it at the normal time around 30 mins. For a creamy with an oozy raw center, bake it at a lesser amount of time around 20 mins. And for a firmer texture, bake it a bit longer than the normal time of 30 mins.

16. Let the cake cool down to room temperature before chilling in the fridge for a few hours or overnight.

17. If you prefer a softer texture with a custard-like filling, take out the cheesecake from the fridge for about 15 to 30 minutes before serving. This will also bring out the flavor of the cream cheese better. But if you prefer a firm texture, then serve it cold.

Total Servings = 6

Nutrition info per serving
Total Carb = 2.4 g Dietary Fiber = 0 Net Carb = 2.4 g
Calories = 287 Total Fat =28.7 g Protein = 6.1 g

Basque Burnt Cheesecake (Chocolate)

INGREDIENTS

Cream Cheese (room temperature) = 400 g / 1 2/3 cups (Note: I used Philadelphia Cream Cheese. It's best to use good quality cream cheese as it is after all, the star of the cake.)

Whole Eggs (room temperature) = 2 large (115 g)

Whipping or Heavy Cream (room temperature) = 220 ml / 1 cup

Powdered Allulose = 130 g / 2/3 cup

Salt = A pinch

Vanilla extract = 1 tsp

Unsweetened cocoa powder (sieved) = 7 g / 1 tbsp

Unsweetened dark chocolate (chopped) = 80 g / 1/2 cup

DIRECTIONS

1. Preheat the oven at 428 F or 200 C. It's best to preheat the oven longer, around 20 to 30 minutes so that it is hot enough. The burnt texture is created by the high temperature and shorter baking time.

2. Melt the dark chocolate in the microwave for 60 seconds, mix then microwave again for 30 seconds. Mix until smooth then set aside.

DIRECTIONS

3. I used a 7 inch (18 cm) pan but you could use a 6 inch (15 cm) pan too except the cake will be thicker. Roughly line with parchment paper and cut off any excess then set aside.

4. It's important to bring the cream cheese, eggs and whipping cream to room temperature so that they blend together easily creating a smoother batter.

5. In a bowl, add the cream cheese and use a spatula to mix until smooth and creamy.

6. Add the sweetener and mix until smooth and creamy.

7. Add the eggs, vanilla extract, salt and whisk until well combined.

8. Add the whipping cream and whisk until smooth and creamy.

9. Add the melted chocolate and cocoa powder then whisk until well combined. The batter is thick and smooth.

10. Transfer into the pan and tap a few times.

11. Bake at the middle rack with top, bottom heat and fan for about 20 to 30 mins. If you only have a conventional oven with regular bake option, then bring the rack higher as heat rises so the upper oven will be hotter. However, if your oven is top heating, make sure that the parchment paper is not touching the heating element to prevent any burning. As all ovens are different, pay attention to the darkening of the top. Rotate the pan midway to ensure even browning. If the top is not darkening fast enough, you may have to give up on the color as you can't keep on baking. Sometimes, you may have to reduce the temperature if the top is burning too fast. So you need to adapt to the situation as every oven is different.

12. Once the top is dark enough, immediately remove the pan. If you wish to have a darker top, just switch to the top heat for a little while before removing the pan. After removing the pan, just give it a jiggle and if the cake is wobbly, then it is done. The texture will firm up as it cools.

13. Do not over bake the cake after 30 mins even if the top is not dark enough as the texture of the cake will be affected.

DIRECTIONS

14. During baking, the cake will rise but will sink down after some time.

15. Whether you prefer a creamy texture or a creamy texture with an oozy raw center or a firmer texture like regular cheesecake, it basically boils down to the baking time. For a creamy texture, bake it at the normal time around 30 mins. For a creamy with an oozy raw center, bake it at a lesser amount of time around 20 mins. And for a firmer texture, bake it a bit longer than the normal time of 30 mins.

16. Let the cake cool down to room temperature before chilling in the fridge for at least 6 hours or overnight.

17. If you prefer a softer texture with a custard-like filling, take out the cheesecake from the fridge for about 15 to 30 minutes before serving. This will also bring out the flavor of the cream cheese better. But if you prefer a firm texture, then serve it cold.

Total Servings = 8

Nutrition info per serving
Total Carb = 5.1 g Dietary Fiber = 1.7 g Net Carb = 3.4 g
Calories = 334 Total Fat =33.2 g Protein = 6.4 g

Berries Muffins

Ingredients

DRY INGREDIENTS
Almond flour = 240 g / 2 cups
Baking powder = 8 g / 2 tsp
Baking soda = 1/4 tsp to 1 tsp (optional)
Monk fruit = 70 g / 1/3 cup
Salt = 2 g / 1/2 tsp

WET INGREDIENTS

Unsweetened Greek Yogurt = 200 g / 0.83 cups
Whole eggs = 4 large (230 g)
Unsalted melted butter = 40 ml / 2 3/4 tbsp
Vanilla extract = 2 tsp

Fresh strawberries (cubed) = 110 g / 2/3 cup
Fresh blueberries (whole)= 100 g / 2/3 cup
Almond flour = 6 g / 1 tbsp
Note:
1.You can also use any other type of berries
2.Mix the berries with the almond flour then set aside. This is to prevent the berries from settling at the bottom.

DIRECTIONS

1.Preheat the oven at 340F or 170C.
2. In a big bowl, add all the wet ingredients and whisk until smooth and creamy.
3. Add all the dry ingredients and mix until well combined.
4. Then add 3/4 of the berries into the batter and mix to combine.
5. Spoon the batter into paper cups up to 3/4 high. Top with remaining berries.
6. Bake for about 15 to 20 minutes or until a wooden skewer comes out clean.
7. This recipe makes about 17 small muffins and 12 medium sized muffins.

Total Servings = 12

Nutrition info per serving
Total Carb = 5.5 g Dietary Fiber = 1.8 g Net Carb = 3.7 g
Calories = 133 Total Fat = 10.8 g Protein = 3.9 g

Berry Crumb Cake

DRY INGREDIENTS

Coconut flour = 60 g / 1/2 cup

(OR Almond Flour = 240 g / 2 cups)

Baking powder = 8 g / 2 tsp

Salt = 4 g / 1 tsp

Monk fruit = 50 g / 1/4 cup

Lemon zest = 1 tbsp

Fresh strawberries (cubed) = 80 g / 1/2 cup

Fresh blueberries (whole) = 80 g / /1/2 cup

Coconut flour = 14 g / 1 tbsp

Note: You can also use any other type of berries

WET INGREDIENTS

Whole eggs = 3 large (170 g)

Whipping cream = 200 ml / 0.8 cup

Unsalted Butter (softened) = 60 g / 1/4 cup

Vanilla extract = 2 tsp

INGREDIENTS FOR TOPPINGS

	Coconut flour	Almond flour
Flour amount	50 g	80 g
Ground cinnamon	1 tbsp.	1/2 tbsp.
Cold Butter (cubed)	50 g	30 g
Monk fruit	50 g	30 g
Walnuts (chopped)	50 g	30 g

DIRECTIONS

1. Preheat the oven to 350F or 180C.

2. In a bowl, mix all the dry ingredients and set aside.

3. In another bowl, whisk the butter and monk fruit until the butter turns into a lighter color. Then add all the wet ingredients and whisk until well combined.

4. Add the dry ingredients and whisk until smooth and thick. Scrape the sides with a spatula and smoothen the batter.

5. Transfer batter into a greased 6 inch (15 cm) square pan with a removable bottom. You can also use a 6 inch or 7-inch (18 cm) spring form pan. Set aside.

6. Meanwhile, prepare the toppings. In a bowl, add the flour, monk fruit and cold butter. Cut the butter with hands until small crumbs are formed. Then add the ground cinnamon and walnuts and mix to combine.

7. Top the batter with the berries.

8. Sprinkle with the toppings until the entire batter is covered.

9. Bake at the middle rack for about 45 to 60 mins or until a wooden skewer comes out clean. If the top is browning too fast, cover with foil.

10. Cool the cake completely before slicing.

Total Servings = 9

Nutrition info per serving (Coconut flour option)
Total Carb = 4.3 g Dietary Fiber = 1.4 g Net Carb = 2.9 g
Calories = 224 Total Fat = 21.9 g Protein = 4.2 g

Nutrition info per serving (Almond flour option)
Total Carb = 8.2 g Dietary Fiber = 3.2 g Net Carb = 5.0 g
Calories = 345 Total Fat = 31.6 g Protein = 8.5 g

Black Sesame Cake

Keto

Ingredients

DRY INGREDIENTS
Coconut flour = 40 g / 1/3 cup
(OR Almond flour = 160 g / 1.3 cups)
Ground Black Sesame Seed = 40 g / 1/3 cup (You can use self-ground or pre ground black sesame seeds)
Baking Powder = 12 g / 3 tsp
Monk fruit = 50 g / 1/4 cup.
Salt = 1/4 to 1/2 tsp

WET INGREDIENTS
Whipping Cream = 200 ml / 0.8 cup
Whole Eggs = 3 large (170 g)
Coconut oil = 60 ml / 1/4 cup

DIRECTIONS

1. Preheat the oven at 340 F or 170 C.

2. In a bowl, add all the dry ingredients and mix until well combined.

3. Add all the wet ingredients and whisk until well combined. The batter is thick and smooth.

4. Transfer the batter into a greased pan lined with parchment paper at the bottom. I used a 6 inch or 15 cm round pan with a removable bottom. You can also use a springform pan or any suitable pan. This cake is quite small so you can easily increase the recipe.

5. Bake at the middle rack for 40 to 50 minutes or until a wooden skewer comes out clean.

6. Cool completely on a wire rack then dust with powdered sweetener (optional).

Total Servings = 8

Nutrition info per serving (Coconut flour option)
Total Carb = 2.2 g Dietary Fiber = 1.0 g Net Carb = 1.2 g Calories = 192 Total Fat = 19.2 g Protein = 4.0 g

Nutrition info per serving (Almond flour option)
Total Carb = 4.6 g Dietary Fiber = 2.1 g Net Carb = 2.5 g Calories = 269 Total Fat = 25.4 g Protein = 6.7 g

Blueberry Cheesecake

INGREDIENTS FOR CRUST

Almond flour = 180 g / 1 1/2 cups (You can also use any ground nuts)

Melted Butter = 50 g / 3 1/4 tbsp (Salted or unsalted is fine)

Monk fruit = 20 g / 2 1/2 tbsp

INGREDIENTS FOR CHEESECAKE

Cream Cheese (softened) = 450 g / 2 cups (I used Philadelphia Original Cream Cheese)

Unsweetened Greek Yogurt = 80 g / 1/3 cup

Whole Eggs = 2 large (115 g)

Monk fruit = 100 g / 1/2 cup

Vanilla extract = 1 tsp

Fresh Blueberries = 150 g / 1 cup (Wash and dried)

(Note: As an option, you can add 1/2 to 1 tsp of xanthan gum if you prefer

the cheesecake texture to be firmer)

INGREDIENTS FOR TOPPING

Fresh Blueberries = 300 g / 2 cups (You can reduce the amount of blueberries to cut down on the carb content)

Monk fruit = 50 g / 1/4 cup

Cold Water = 40 ml / 2 3/4 tbsp

Fresh lemon juice = 1 tbsp

Butter = 14 g / 1 tbsp (Salted or unsalted is fine)

Xanthan Gum = 1/4 tsp

DIRECTIONS

1. Preheat the oven at 325F or 160C.

2. In a bowl, add the almond flour, monk fruit and mix to combine. Then add the melted butter and mix until crumbly. Even though it looks crumbly but when you squeeze it, it will look like a firm dough. Transfer into a 7-inch (18 cm) springform pan, greased and lined with parchment paper at the bottom. You can also use an 8-inch (20 cm) springform pan in which case, the cheesecake will be slightly flatter. Use your hands to spread the dough evenly. It should cover the sides of the pan slightly. Baking the crust is optional. I prefer to bake it for only 10 minutes at 350F or 180C so that the crust is drier. But it is totally up to you. Set aside.

3. In another bowl, add the softened cream cheese and use a spatula to mix until creamy. Then add the sweetener and mix to combine. Switch to a whisk and mix until smooth and creamy. You can use a handheld whisk or stand mixer but there will be more cleaning to do.

4. Add the yogurt and vanilla extract and whisk to combine.

5. Add the eggs one at a time and whisk to combine.

6. Finally, add the fresh blueberries and use a spatula to mix until well combined.

7. Pour the batter onto the crust and spread evenly.

DIRECTIONS

8. Bake at 325F or 160C for 35 to 40 minutes. It is done when the top feels slightly springy and firm.

9. Let the cheesecake come to room temperature then wrap with foil (do not remove the pan) and chill for at least 6 hours or preferably overnight.

10. Just before serving, make the blueberry topping. In a small pan, add the sweetener, xanthan gum, water and whisk until dissolved. Then add half the blueberries, lemon juice and stir constantly until it becomes a thick and jammy consistency. Cook over a low to medium heat.

11. Remove pan from heat, add the balance of blueberries, butter and stir until the butter is dissolved. Transfer into a bowl and chill until it gets to room temperature or slightly cooler is fine too.

12. Remove the foil from the cheesecake (do not remove the pan yet). Spoon the blueberry topping onto the surface of the cheesecake then remove the pan.

13. Serve immediately or you can chill it for a while before serving.

Total Servings = 12

Nutrition info per serving
Total Carb = 9.0 g Dietary Fiber = 2.1 g Net Carb = 6.9
g Calories = 260 Total Fat = 22.3 g Protein = 6.9 g

Blueberry Muffins

Ingredients

DRY NGREDIENTS
Coconut flour = 90 g / 3/4 cup

Other flour options :
1. Almond flour = 360 g / 3 cups
2. Almond flour = 180 g / 1 1/2 cups +
Coconut flour = 45 g / 6 1/2 tbsp

Monk fruit = 100 g / 1/2 cup.
Baking Powder = 8 g / 2 tsp
Salt = 1/4 tsp

Fresh blueberries = 150 / 3/4 cup (Mix with 7 g / 1 tbsp of Coconut flour. This is to prevent all the blueberries from settling at the bottom. Set aside)

WET NGREDIENTS

Whole eggs = 5 large (290 g)
Whipping cream = 240 ml / 1 cup
Coconut oil = 60 ml / 1/4 cup
Vanilla extract = 1 tsp

DIRECTIONS

1. Preheat the oven at 340F or 170C.
2. In a bowl, mix all the dry ingredients (except the blueberries) until well combined.
3. Add all the wet ingredients and mix to combine. The batter is thick and smooth.
4. Add the blueberries but reserve some for toppings.
5. Scoop the batter into the paper cups until 3/4 high. I used small and firm paper cups (about 50 g each) so I got 12 servings.
6. Add the reserved blueberries on the top of the batter.
7. Bake for 25 minutes or until a wooden skewer comes out clean.

Total Servings = 12

Nutrition info per serving
Total Carb = 2.9 g Dietary Fiber = 0.7 g Net Carb = 2.2 g Calories = 93 Total Fat = 8.0 g Protein = 2.6 g

Butter Cake

INGREDIENTS

Coconut Flour = 90 g / 3/4 cup
(OR Almond Flour = 300 g / 2 1/2 cup)

Baking Powder = 8 g / 2 tsp

Unsalted Butter (Room Temperature) = 225 g / 1 cup

Salt = 4 g / 1 tsp (If using salted butter, you can omit the salt)

Monk fruit = 100 g / 1/2 cup

Whole Eggs = 4 large (230 g)

Vanilla Extract = 1 tsp

DIRECTIONS

1. Preheat the oven at 350F or 180C.

2. In a bowl, beat the butter and monk fruit at medium to high speed until light and fluffy. Scrape the sides intermittently.

3. Add the eggs one at a time and whisk to combine.

4. Add the vanilla extract and whisk to combine.

5. Add the coconut or almond flour, baking powder, salt and whisk at low speed to combine. The batter should be smooth and thick.

6. Transfer the batter into an 8x4 inch (20x10 cm) loaf pan lined with parchment paper. Spread evenly.

7. Bake for 40 mins for the coconut flour version and 55 mins for the almond flour version as the loaf is bigger. It is done when a wooden skewer comes out clean.

8. If the top is browning too fast, cover with foil.

9. Once the cake is done, rest it upside down for 15 minutes. This is to prevent the butter from settling at the bottom. After resting, turnover and slice the cake accordingly.

Total Servings = 15

Nutrition info per serving (Coconut flour version)
Total Carb =0.8 g Dietary Fiber = 0.3 g Net Carb = 0.5
g Calories = 128 g Total Fat = 13.5 g Protein = 1.7 g

Nutrition info per serving (Almond flour version)
Total Carb = 4.6 g Dietary Fiber = 2.1 g Net Carb = 2.5
g
Calories = 238 Total Fat = 23.2 g Protein = 5.9 g

Butter Cake - Almond & Coconut
(Short Cut Version)

Ingredients

DRY INGREDIENTS
Almond flour = 150 g / 1 1/4 cup
Coconut flour = 40 g / 5 3/4 tbsp
Baking Powder = 12 g / 3 tsp
Monk fruit = 80 g / 6 1/3 tbsp
Salt = 3/4 to 1 tsp

WET INGREDIENTS
Unsalted Melted Butter (room temperature) = 225 g / 1
cup Whole eggs (room temperature) = 4 large (230 g)
Vanilla Extract = 1 tsp

DIRECTIONS

1. Preheat the oven at 350 F or 180 C.

2. In a bowl, add all the wet ingredients and whisk until well combined. Set aside.

3. In a separate bowl, add all the dry ingredients and mix until well combined.

4. Add the wet into the dry ingredients and whisk until well combined. The batter is thick and smooth.

5. Pour the batter into a greased 6-inch (15 cm) round pan with a removable bottom. Line with parchment paper at the bottom. You can also use an 8x4 inch (20x10cm) loaf pan lightly greased and lined with parchment paper. Spread evenly.

6. Bake at the middle rack for 60 minutes or until a wooden skewer comes out clean. If you use an 8x4 inch loaf pan, the baking time will be slightly shorter around 45 to 55 minutes. 7. If the top is browning too fast, cover with foil.

8. Once ready, cool for 15 minutes then remove the cake from the pan. As an option, you can rest the cake upside down for 15 minutes as this will help to prevent the butter from settling at the bottom. Then turn over and slice accordingly.

Total Servings = 12

Nutrition info per serving
Total Carb = 2.2 g Dietary Fiber = 1.1 g Net Carb = 1.1 g
Calories = 207 g Total Fat = 20.7 g Protein = 3.9 g

Butter Cake - Almond
(Short Cut Version)

Ingredients

DRY INGREDIENTS
Almond flour = 300 g / 2 1/2 cups
Baking Powder = 12 g / 3 tsps
Monk fruit = 100 g / 1/2 cup
Salt = 3/4 to 1 tsp

WET INGREDIENTS
Unsalted Melted Butter (room temperature) = 225 g / 1 cup
Whole eggs (room temperature) = 4 large (230 g)
Vanilla Extract = 1 tsp

DIRECTIONS

1.. Preheat the oven at 350 F or 180 C.

2. In a bowl, add all the wet ingredients and whisk until well combined. Set aside.

3. In a separate bowl, add all the dry ingredients and mix until well combined.

4. Add the wet into the dry ingredients and whisk until well combined. The batter is smooth and thick.

5. Transfer the batter into a greased 8x4 inch (20x10 cm) loaf pan lined with parchment paper at the bottom. I used an 8x4 inch silicone loaf pan lightly greased with butter. Spread evenly.

6. Bake at the middle rack for 45 to 55 minutes or until a wooden skewer comes out clean.

7. If the top is browning too fast, cover with foil.

8. Once ready, remove from the pan and let the cake rest upside down for 15 minutes. This is to prevent the butter from settling at the bottom.

9. After 15 minutes, turn over and slice accordingly. .

Total Servings = 16

Nutrition info per serving
Total Carb = 2.8 g Dietary Fiber = 1.3 g Net Carb = 1.5 g
Calories = 192 g Total Fat = 18.4 g Protein = 4.2 g

Butter Cake - Coconut
(Short Cut Version)

Ingredients

DRY INGREDIENTS
Coconut flour = 90 g / 3/4 cup
Baking Powder = 12 g / 3 tsp
Monk fruit = 70 g / 1/3 cup
Salt = 1/2 tsp

WET INGREDIENTS
Unsalted Melted Butter (room temperature) = 225 g / 1
cup Whole eggs (room temperature) = 4 large (230 g)
Vanilla Extract = 1 tsp

DIRECTIONS

1. Preheat the oven at 350 F or 180 C.
2. In a bowl, add all the wet ingredients and whisk until well combined. Set aside.
3. In a separate bowl, add all the dry ingredients and mix until well combined.
4. Add the wet into the dry ingredients and whisk until well combined. The batter is smooth and thick.
5. Transfer the batter into a greased 8x4 inch (20x10 cm) loaf pan lined with parchment paper at the bottom. I used an 8x4 inch silicone loaf pan lightly greased with butter. Spread evenly.
6. Bake at the middle rack for 45 to 55 minutes or until a wooden skewer comes out clean.
7. If the top is browning too fast, cover with foil.
8. Once ready, remove from the pan and let the cake rest upside down for 15 minutes. This is to prevent the butter from settling at the bottom.
9. After 15 minutes, turn over and slice accordingly.

Total Servings = 16

Nutrition info per serving
Total Carb = 2.8 g Dietary Fiber = 1.3 g Net Carb = 1.5 g
Calories = 192 g Total Fat = 18.4 g Protein = 4.2 g

Carrot Cake - Ground Sunflower Seeds
(With Eggless Option)

DRY INGREDIENTS

Ground raw sunflower seeds = 240 g / 2 cups

Baking powder = 12 g / 3 tsp

Salt = 4 g / 1 tsp

Monk fruit = 70 g / 1/3 cup

Ground cinnamon = 5 g / 2 tsp

Ground allspice = 4 g / 2 tsp

Grated carrots = 86 g / 3/4 cup (Plus a bit more for garnishing - optional)

Roasted & chopped walnuts = 60 g / 1/2 cup (For nut free option, omit this or replace with roasted seeds)

WET INGREDIENTS

Whole Eggs = 3 large (170 g) (See below for eggless option)

Coconut oil = 40 g / 2.7 tbsp

Whipping cream = 80 g / 5 1/2 tbsp

EGGLESS VERSION

1. You can replace the eggs with 3 flax eggs ;
In a bowl, mix together 21 g / 3 tbsp of ground flaxseeds or flax meal + 135 ml / 9 tbsp of water. Let it rest until thickened before using.

2. I used an 8 inch (20 cm) square pan and even though the batter is much lower in height but it still took 50 minutes to cook at the same temperature of 340F or 170C. Hence, I suggest that you use a bigger pan otherwise, it will be quite hard to cook through if using a 6 inch (15 cm) pan.

3. The texture is softer, stickier and a little fragile but tastes just as good.

DIRECTIONS

1. Preheat the oven at 340F or 170C.

2. In a bowl, add all the dry ingredients and mix until well combined.

3. Add all the wet ingredients and mix until well combined. The batter is quite thick.

4. Transfer the batter into a 6 inch (15 cm) pan with a removable bottom. Grease and line the pan with parchment paper. Spread evenly.

5. Bake for 50 to 60 minutes or until a wooden skewer comes out clean.

6. Cool completely.

7. Before frosting, trim off the uneven top of the cake.

8. Scoop the cream cheese frosting onto the top and side of cake. Spread evenly.

9. Sprinkle with grated carrots on the edge of the cake and top with chopped and roasted walnuts.

INGREDIENTS FOR CREAM CHEESE FROSTING

Softened cream cheese (brick style) = 225 g / 8 oz
Powdered sweetener = 50 g / 7 tbsp
Lemon zest = zest from 1 lemon (optional)

DIRECTIONS

1. In a bowl, mix the softened cream cheese with a spatula until creamy.
2. Add the powdered sweetener and mix until smooth and creamy.
3. Add the lemon zest (if using) and mix to combine.
4. Chill until needed.

Total Servings = 8

Nutrition info per serving
Total Carb = 4.5 g Dietary Fiber = 2.0 g Net Carb = 2.5 g
Calories = 280 g Total Fat = 26.5 g Protein = 7.7 g

Carrot Muffins

Ingredients

DRY INGREDIENTS
Almond flour = 360 g / 3 cups
Baking powder = 8 g / 2 tsp
Baking soda = 4 g / 1 tsp (optional)
Ground cinnamon = 7 1/2 g / 3 tsp
All spice = 6 g / 3 tsp
Monk fruit = 50 g / 1/4 cup
Grated carrots = 135 g / 1 1/2 cups
Chopped roasted walnuts = 60 g / 1/2 cup

WET INGREDIENTS
Whole Eggs = 6 large (345 g)
Unsalted Melted Butter = 60 ml / 1/4 cup
Unsweetened Greek Yogurt = 300 g / 1.2 cups

DIRECTIONS

1. Preheat the oven at 350F or 180C.

2. In a bowl, add all the dry ingredients (except the grated carrots and chopped walnuts) and mix with a spatula until well combined.

3. Add the wet into the dry ingredients and whisk until well combined.

4. Lastly, add the grated carrots, chopped walnuts and mix until well combined.

5. Scoop into paper cups until 3/4 high and bake for 15 to 20 minutes or until a wooden skewer comes out clean.

6. Let the muffins cool completely, then pipe the cream cheese frosting on top. Sprinkle with grated carrots (optional).

INGREDIENTS FOR CREAM CHEESE FROSTING

Softened cream cheese (brick style) = 225 g / 8 oz

Powdered sweetener = 100 g / 1/2 cup

Lemon zest = zest from 1 lemon (optional)

DIRECTIONS

1. In a bowl, mix the softened cream cheese with a spatula until creamy. 2. Add the powdered sweetener and mix until smooth and creamy.

3. Add the lemon zest (if using) and mix to combine.

4. Chill until needed.

Total Servings = 12

Nutrition info per serving
Total Carb = 7.2 g Dietary Fiber = 2.5 g Net Carb = 4.7
g Calories = 290 g Total Fat = 24.8 g Protein = 10.0 g

Cheddar Cheese Butter Cake

INGREDIENTS

Almond flour = 360 g / 3 cups
(OR Coconut flour = 90 g / 3/4 cup.
Unsalted Butter (room temperature) = 225 g / 1 cup
Baking Powder = 8 g / 2 tsp
Salt = 3 g / 3/4 tsp (Note: If you used salted butter, then you may omit the salt)
Whole Eggs = 4 large (230 g)
Powdered sweetener= 100 g / 1/2 cup
Vanilla Extract = 2 tsp
Shredded Cheddar Cheese = 120 g / 1.45 cup (Note: I used a mix of half regular cheddar and half sharp cheddar. If you like a stronger cheese flavor, you can also use any stronger grated cheese).

DIRECTIONS

1. Preheat the oven at 340F or 170C.
2. In a bowl, add the butter and sweetener. Beat at medium high speed with a handheld or stand mixer until light and fluffy.
3. Add the eggs one at a time and whisk to combine.
4. Add the vanilla extract and whisk to combine.
5. Add the flour, salt, baking powder and whisk to combine. Switch to a spatula and mix thoroughly until thick and smooth.
6. Add the shredded cheese and mix until well combined.
7. Roughly line an 8-inch (or 20 cm) round pan with parchment paper for a rustic look. This also makes it easier to handle the grease. You can also use any other suitable pan but do not use too small and narrow pan as it will be more difficult to cook the cake properly.
8. Scoop the batter into the pan and spread evenly.
9. Bake for 40 to 50 minutes or until cooked. Test with a wooden skewer. If the top of the cake is browning too fast, cover with foil.
10. Let cool then remove the cake from the pan.

Total Servings = 12

Nutrition info per serving (Almond flour version)
Total Carb = 4.5 g Dietary Fiber = 2.1 g Net Carb = 2.4 g
Calories = 316 g Total Fat = 29.5 g Protein = 8.8 g

Nutrition info per serving (Coconut flour version)
Total Carb = 1.1 g Dietary Fiber = 0.4 g Net Carb = 0.7 g
Calories =199 g Total Fat = 20 g Protein = 4.3 g

Cheese Muffins

Ingredients

DRY INGREDIENTS

Almond flour = 240 g / 2 cups

Other flour options:

1. Ground Sunflower Seeds = 240 g / 2 cups

2. Coconut flour = 60 g / 1/2 cup

Baking Powder = 8 g / 2 tsp

Salt = 1/2 tsp

Black Pepper = 1 tsp

Monk fruit = 12 g / 1 tbsp (optional)

Grated or Shredded Cheese = 200 g / 2 cups (Note: I used 150 g cheddar and 50 g sharp cheddar cheese)

WET INGREDIENTS

Unsweetened Pea Milk = 240 mil / 1 cup (You can also use unsweetened almond milk or any other keto friendly milk)

Whole Eggs = 2 large (115 g)

Unsalted Melted Butter = 60 ml / 1/4 cup

NOTE

1. For coconut flour, the amount of milk should be reduced to 180 ml / 3/4 cup.
2. For ground sunflower seeds, the amount of milk should be reduced to 120 ml / 1/2 cup.

TOPPING

Paprika powder

More shredded cheese

DIRECTIONS

1. Preheat the oven at 320F or 160C.
2. In a bowl, whisk all the wet ingredients until well combined then set aside.
3. In a separate bowl, mix all the dry ingredients until well combined.
4. Add the wet into the dry ingredients and mix to combine until a thick batter is formed.

DIRECTIONS

5. I used a silicone mold as it is so easy to remove the muffins. You can also use firm paper cups or muffin tins. It's normal for the muffins to rise well then subsequently deflate at the middle. To avoid this, use shallow or small paper cups. If you are using big paper cups, try to fill it halfway only.

6. Spoon the batter into the mold.

7. Sprinkle it with paprika powder then top with more cheese.

8. Bake for 20 to 25 mins or until golden brown.

9. You can enjoy these cheese muffins with coffee, serve it with salad or as a side.

10. These cheese muffins can be reheated with a mini oven toaster or microwave. But to get a crispy top, it's best to use an oven toaster.

11. These cheese muffins can be refrigerated for up to a week and frozen for up to 3 months.

Total Servings = 14

Nutrition info per serving (Almond flour version)
Total Carb = 4.0 g Dietary Fiber = 1.9 g Net Carb = 2.1 g
Calories = 197 g Total Fat = 17.6 g Protein = 8.1 g

Total Servings = 10

Nutrition info per serving (Coconut flour version)
Total Carb = 1.0 g Dietary Fiber = 0.4 g Net Carb = 0.6 g
Calories = 144 g Total Fat = 12.9 g Protein = 6.4 g

Total Servings = 12

Nutrition info per serving (Gd Sunflower Seed version)
Total Carb = 2.0 g Dietary Fiber = 0.7 g Net Carb = 1.3 g
Calories =152 g Total Fat = 13.6 g Protein = 6.6 g

Cheesecake Bars

INGREDIENTS FOR CRUST
Ground almond or any nuts = 180 g / 1 1/2 cups
Monk fruit = 25 g / 2 tbsp
Melted Unsalted Butter = 70 g / 5 tbsp
Salt = 1/8 tsp (optional)

INGREDIENTS FOR CHEESECAKE
Cream Cheese (brick style) = 680 g / 24 oz
(softened) Powdered Sweetener = 200 g / 1 1/2 cups
Sour Cream = 120 g / 1/2 cup
Whole Eggs (room temperture) = 3 large (170 g)
Vanilla extract = 1 tsp
Salt = 1/4 tsp (optional)

INGREDIENTS FOR GANACHE
Unsweetened dark chocolate = 117 g / 1/3 cup (chopped)
Heavy or whipping cream = 120 ml / 1/2 cup
(Note: As an option, you can add sweetener to balance out the bitterness
from the ganache. You can also use sugar free dark chocolate that has been
been sweetened with stevia)

DIRECTIONS

1. Preheat the oven at 325F or 165C.

2. To make the crust, mix the ground almond, monkfruit, salt (if using) in a bowl until combined. Then add the melted butter and mix until crumbly. Transfer to a 9x9 inch (23 cm) square pan lined with parchment paper. Spread evenly and set aside. As an option, you can pre-bake the crust at 350F or 180C for 10 to 15 minutes for a crispier texture.

3. To make the cheesecake, add the softened cream cheese, powdered sweetener, salt (if using) and use a handheld or stand mixer to beat at medium speed until creamy. Then add the sour cream, vanilla extract and beat to combine. Add the eggs one at a time, beat at low speed to combine. The batter is smooth and creamy. Pour over the crust and spread evenly. Bake for 30 to 40 minutes or until just set. The sides may puff up and the center a little jiggly which is normal. After baking, cool until room temperature then wrap with foil and refrigerate for 5 to 6 hours or preferably overnight.

4. After the cheesecake is properly chilled, make the ganache. Heat the heavy or whipping cream in microwave or stove top until the sides are simmering. Pour over the chopped chocolate. Cover with foil for 5 minutes, then whisk until smooth and creamy. Remove the foil from the cheesecake and spoon the ganache over the surface of the cheesecake. Spread evenly then chill until the ganache is set. Cut into 12 or 16 servings. Clean the knife after each cut.

Total Servings = 16

Nutrition info per serving
Total Carb = 5.7 g Dietary Fiber = 1.8 g Net Carb = 3.9 g Calories = 315 g Total Fat = 31.1 g Protein = 7.1 g

Cheesecake Brownie

INGREDIENTS FOR FUDGY BROWNIE

Unsweetened chocolate = 175 g / 1 cup (Note: I used Baker's Unsweetened Dark Chocolate, but you can use any suitable chocolate)

Unsalted Butter (room temperature) = 113 g / 1/2 cup

Monk fruit = 120 g / 1/2 cup

Unsweetened Cocoa Powder (sieved) = 30 g / 1/4 cup

Coconut flour = 30 g / 1/4 cup

(OR Almond flour = 120 g / 1 cup)

(OR Ground Sunflower Seeds) = 120 g / 1 cup)

Whole Eggs = 3 large (170 g)

Salt = 1/2 tsp

Almond Nibs = 50 g / 0.6 cup (This is optional. You can also use any other nuts, chocolate chips or just leave it plain)

INGREDIENTS FOR CHEESECAKE

Cream Cheese (softened) = 450 g / 16 oz

Monk fruit = 100 g / 1/2 cup

Whole Eggs = 2 large (115 g)

Vanilla Extract = 2 tsp

DIRECTIONS FOR BROWNIE

1. Preheat the oven at 350F or 180C.

2. Melt the butter and chocolate in a bowl over the stove at low heat. You can also use the microwave to melt at intervals. Once the chocolate is almost melted, turn off the heat and just stir until it is melted. Remove pan from the stove. Do not overheat the mixture as it can cause the chocolate to split resulting in the fat seeping out from the cocoa butter.

3. Add the sweetener and whisk until combined.

4. Add the eggs one at a time and whisk to combine until the texture is smooth and thick.

5. Add the salt, sieved cocoa powder and whisk until combined.

6. Add the coconut flour and fold with a spatula until well combined.

7. Reserve 120 g / 1 cup of the batter and set aside.

8. Add the almond nibs (if using) and mix to combine.

9. Transfer batter into a greased 9-inch (23 cm) pan lined with parchment paper. Spread evenly and chill in the fridge while preparing the cheesecake.

DIRECTIONS FOR CHEESECAKE

1. Beat the cream cheese with a handheld mixer until light and fluffy (about 3 to 5 mins at medium speed).
2. Add the sweetener, vanilla extract and beat until combined.
3. Add the eggs, one at a time and beat until combined.
4. Pour over the brownie layer.
5. Mix 1 to 1 1/2 tbsp of hot water with the reserved brownie batter and stir until smooth. This is to thin out the batter so that it's easier to swirl to create the marble effect.
6. Use a wooden skewer to swirl around to create a marble effect.
7. Bake for about 30 minutes. The center may feel a little spongy but it is fine as it will firm up when cooled. Overbaking will make the cake drier.
8. Cool completely then remove from the pan and cut into 25 servings. If you prefer, you can cut them into bigger squares.

Total Servings = 25

Nutrition info per serving
Total Carb = 4.3 g Dietary Fiber = 2.2 g Net Carb = 2.1 g
Calories = 165 g Total Fat = 15.9 g Protein = 4.3 g

Chocolate Butter Cake

Ingredients

DRY INGREDIENTS
Almond Flour = 300 g / 2 1/2 cups
(OR Coconut Flour = 90 g / 3/4 cup)
Baking Powder = 10 g / 2 1/2 tsp
Unsweetened Cocoa Powder = 40 g / 1/3 cup
Salt = 1/2 tsp

Unsalted Butter (Softened) = 300 g / 1 1/3 cup
Monk fruit = 120 g / 0.6 cup
Whole Eggs = 4 large (230 g)
Vanilla Extract = 2 tsp

DIRECTIONS

1. Preheat the oven at 350F or 180C.

2. In a bowl, add all the dry ingredients and mix until well combined. Set aside.

3. In a separate bowl, beat the butter and sweetener at medium to high speed until light and fluffy. Scrape the sides intermittently.

4. Add the eggs one at a time and whisk to combine.

5. Add the vanilla extract and whisk to combine.

6. Add the dry ingredients gradually and whisk to combine. Then use a spatula to mix thoroughly. The batter should be smooth and thick.

7. Transfer the batter into an 8 1/2 x 4 1/2 inch (20x10 cm) loaf pan greased and lined with parchment paper and spread evenly. You can also use a 9 x 5 inch (23x13 cm) loaf pan or any bigger pan in square, rectangular or round shapes which will actually cook faster to prevent over browning as chocolate can burn quite easily. You can even make them into cupcakes.

8. Bake for 50 to 60 mins or until cooked. If you use a bigger pan, it will require less cooking time. Just test with a wooden skewer. Cover with foil midway to prevent over browning.

10. Once ready, remove from the pan and let the cake rest upside down for 15 minutes. This is to prevent the butter from settling at the bottom.

9. After 15 minutes, turn over and slice accordingly.

Total Servings = 15

Nutrition info per serving (Almond flour version)
Total Carb = 4.7 g Dietary Fiber = 2.3 g Net Carb = 2.4 g
Calories = 247 g Total Fat = 24.1 g Protein = 5.0 g

Nutrition info per serving (Coconut flour version)
Total Carb = 2.3 g Dietary Fiber = 1.2 g Net Carb = 1.1 g
Calories = 171 g Total Fat = 17.9 g Protein = 2.3 g

Chocolate Butter Cake - Almond & Coconut
(Short Cut Version)

Ingredients

DRY INGREDIENTS
Almond flour = 150 g / 1 1/4 cup
Coconut flour = 40 g / 5 3/4 tbsp
Unsweetened cocoa powder (sieved) = 30 g / 4 tbsp
Baking Powder = 12 g / 3 tsp
Monk fruit = 100 g / 1/2 cup
Salt = 4 g / 1 tsp

WET INGREDIENTS
Unsalted Melted Butter (room temperature) = 280 g / 1 1/4 cup
Whole eggs (room temperature) = 5 large / 290 g
Vanilla Extract = 1 tsp

DIRECTIONS

1. Preheat the oven at 350 F or 180 C.

2. In a bowl, add all the wet ingredients and whisk until well combined. Set aside.

3. In a separate bowl, add all the dry ingredients and mix until well combined.

4. Add the wet into the dry ingredients and whisk until well combined. The batter is thick and smooth.

5. Transfer the batter into an 8 x 2 inch (20x5 cm) square pan lined with parchment paper and spread evenly. I find that using a square pan shortens the baking time so the cake will be moister and also prevent the crust from hardening. So instead of the usual 50 to 60 minutes baking time, this took only 35 minutes. I set the digital timer at 15 mins then cover the top with foil for the next 15 mins and finally remove the foil and bake for another 5 minutes and it's done. Of course, you can use a loaf pan, round or any suitable pan. However, the baking time will depend on what type of pan you use and how thick is the batter. Always test with a wooden skewer for doneness.

6. Once ready, cool for a while then remove the parchment paper. As an option, you can rest the cake upside down for 15 minutes as this will help to prevent the butter from settling at the bottom. Then turn over and slice accordingly. I cut the cake into 16 squares, but you can choose to cut them bigger or smaller.

7. The cake can be served warm. To reheat, just microwave for 30 seconds for a warm, soft and fluffy texture.

Total Servings = 16

Nutrition info per serving
Total Carb = 2.7 g Dietary Fiber = 1.4 g Net Carb = 1.3 g
Calories = 188 g Total Fat = 18.8 g Protein = 3.6 g

Chocolate Butter Cake - Gd Sunflower Seed (Short Cut Version)

Ingredients

DRY INGREDIENTS
Ground Sunflower Seeds = 360 g / 3 cups
Unsweetened cocoa powder (sieved) = 35 g / 4 3/4 tbsp
Baking Powder = 12 g / 3 tsp
Monk fruit = 100 g / 1/2 cup
Salt = 4 g / 1 tsp

WET INGREDIENTS
Unsalted Melted Butter (room temperature) = 280 g / 1 1/4 cup
Whole eggs (room temperature) = 5 large / 290 g
Vanilla Extract = 2 tsp

DIRECTIONS

1. Preheat the oven at 340 F or 170 C.
2. In a bowl, add all the wet ingredients and whisk until well combined. Set aside.
3. In a separate bowl, add all the dry ingredients and mix until well combined.
4. Add the wet into the dry ingredients and whisk until well combined. The batter is thick and smooth.
5. Transfer the batter into an 8 inch (20 cm) square pan lined with parchment paper and spread evenly. Of course, you can use a loaf pan, round or any suitable pan. However, the baking time will depend on what type of pan you use and how thick is the batter. Always test with a wooden skewer for doneness.
6. Once ready, cool for a while then remove the parchment paper. As an option, you can rest the cake upside down for 15 minutes as this will help to prevent the butter from settling at the bottom. Then turn over and slice accordingly. I cut the cake into 16 squares but you can choose to cut them bigger or smaller.
7. The cake can be served warm. To reheat, just microwave for 30 seconds for a warm, soft and fluffy texture.

Total Servings = 16

Nutrition info per serving
Total Carb = 2.7 g Dietary Fiber = 1.4 g Net Carb = 1.3 g
Calories = 188 g Total Fat = 19.2 g Protein = 3.9 g

Chocolate Cake

Ingredients

DRY INGREDIENTS
Coconut flour = 60 g / 1/2 cup
(OR Almond flour = 240 g / 2 cups)
Baking Powder = 8 g / 2 tsp
Unsweetened Cocoa Powder = 20 g / 2 3/4 tbsp
Monk fruit = 80 g / 6 1/3 tbsp
Salt = 1/2 tsp

WET INGREDIENTS
Whipping Cream = 200 ml / 1 cup
Whole Eggs = 4 large (230 g)
Coconut oil = 80 ml / 5.7 tbsp
Vanilla extract = 10 ml / 2 tsp

DIRECTIONS

1. Preheat the oven at 340F or 170 C.
2. In a bowl, add all the wet ingredients and whisk until well combined. Set aside.
3. In another bowl, sieve the flour, cocoa powder and baking powder. Add the sweetener, salt and mix until well combined.
4. Add the wet ingredients into the dry ingredients and whisk until the batter is thick and smooth.
5. Transfer the batter into a greased pan lined with parchment paper at the bottom. I used a 6 inch or 15 cm round pan with a removable bottom. You can also use a springform pan or any suitable pan. This cake is quite small so you can easily increase the recipe.
6. Bake at the middle rack for 40 to 50 mins or until a wooden skewer comes out clean. For the almond flour version, you may need to bake it longer as it has slightly more volume.
7. Cool completely on a wire rack.
8. Dust with powdered sweetener (optional).

Total Servings = 8

Nutrition info per serving (Coconut flour version)
Total Carb = 2.8 g Dietary Fiber = 1.3 g Net Carb = 1.5 g
Calories = 178 g Total Fat = 17.9 g Protein = 3.5 g

Nutrition info per serving (Almond flour version)
Total Carb = 6.5 g Dietary Fiber = 3.1 g Net Carb = 3.4 g
Calories = 294 g Total Fat = 27.3 g Protein = 7.7 g

Chocolate Cake With Buttercream

Ingredients

DRY INGREDIENTS
Coconut flour = 90 g / 3/4 cup
Baking powder = 12 g / 3 tsp
Baking soda = 4 g / 1 tsp
Salt = 4 g / 1 tsp
Monk fruit = 100 g / 1/2 cup
Cocoa powder (unsweetened) = 45 g / 6 tbsp

WET INGREDIENTS
Whole eggs = 6 large (345 g)
Whipping cream = 315 ml / 1 1/3 cup
Unsalted Melted butter = 100 ml / 1/2 cup

BUTTERCREAM FROSTING

Unsalted Butter (room temperature) = 225 g / 1 cup

Powdered sweetener = 1 1/2 cup

Whipping or heavy cream = 2 tbsp.

Salt = 1 tsp

Cocoa powder (unsweetened) = 20 g / 2.7 tbsp

Garnishing = 1 whole strawberry for each square of cake (optional) or to reduce carb content, you could top with sliced strawberries.

DIRECTIONS FOR CAKE

1. Preheat oven at 340F or 170C.
2. In a bowl, mix all dry ingredients until well combined.
3. Add the wet ingredients and mix until thick and smooth.
4. Transfer batter into a 12 inch (30 cm) square pan lined with parchment paper and spread evenly.
5. Bake for 20 mins or until a wooden skewer comes out clean.
6. Cool cake completely before frosting.

DIRECTIONS FOR BUTTERCREAM FROSTING

1. In a bowl, beat the butter with a handheld mixer until the color turns lighter.
2. Add the powdered sweetener, cocoa powder and whisk until well combined, smooth and creamy.
3. Add the whipping cream, salt and whisk until well combined and smooth.
4. Chill until ready for use.

ASSEMBLE CAKE

1. Cut the cake into half. Gently place half the cake on a tray.
2. Spoon half the cream on top of the cake and spread evenly.
3. Stack the other half of cake on top.
4. Spoon balance of cream on top and spread evenly.
5. Cut the cake to your preferred size. I cut into 10 big squares but you could cut into smaller squares for portion control.
6. Top each square of cake with a whole or sliced strawberry.

Total Servings = 10

Nutrition info per serving
Total Carb = 6.6 g Dietary Fiber = 2.9 g Net Carb = 3.7 g
Calories = 229 g Total Fat = 21.9 g Protein = 5.7 g

Chocolate Cake With Chocolate Ganache

Ingredients

DRY INGREDIENTS
Almond flour = 180 g / 1 1/4 cups
Coconut flour = 45 g / 5 3/4 tbsp
Unsweetened cocoa powder = 38 g / 5 tbsp
Baking powder = 8 g / 2 tsp
Baking soda = 4 g / 1 tsp
Monk fruit = 250 g / 1 1/4 cups (This is mild to moderately sweet so you can increase the amount according to your preference.

WET INGREDIENTS
Whipping Cream = 290 ml / 1.2 cups
Whole eggs = 6 large (345 g)
Coconut oil = 120 ml / 1/2 cup
Vanilla extract = 1 tbsp
(Espresso powder = 5 g / 1 tbsp (Optional

CHOCOLATE GANACHE

Unsweetened dark chocolate (chopped) = 375 g / 2 1/4 cups (I used Baker's Unsweetened Dark Chocolate)
Whipping cream = 240 ml / 1 cup

Note:

1. For a softer texture, you can add another 1/2 to 1 cup of whipping or heavy cream.
2. You can add some powdered sweetener, liquid stevia or use dark chocolate sweetened with stevia)

DIRECTIONS

1. Preheat the oven at 325F or 160C.
2. In a bowl, add all the wet ingredients, whisk until well combined then set aside.
3. In a separate bowl, sieve the almond, coconut flour, cocoa powder, baking powder and soda. Then add the sweetener and salt. Mix until well combined.
4. Add the wet ingredients and whisk until well combined. The batter is thick and smooth.
5. Use a 3x8 inch (20 cm) round pans, greased and lined with parchment paper at the bottom.

DIRECTIONS

6. Divide the batter equally. Spread evenly and tap a few times to
remove air bubbles.
7. Bake for 20 minutes or until a wooden skewer comes out clean.
8. Cool for 5 minutes then remove the pan and parchment paper. Cool
the cake completely on a wire rack.
9. Meanwhile, make the chocolate ganache. Heat the whipping cream in a microwave for 60 seconds then pour onto the chopped chocolate. Mix until the chocolate is melted. This ganache is quite thick but if you
prefer a softer texture, just add more whipping or heavy cream (about
1/2 to 1 cup).
10. Once the cakes are cooled, frost each layer evenly including the top and sides.
11. Use a cake scraper to smoothen the sides then make a design for the sides with a cake scraper with teeth edge. It's super easy and makes the cake look nicer. Then decorate the top with some fresh strawberries and raspberries (optional).

Total Servings = 12

Nutrition info per serving
Total Carb = 12.0 g Dietary Fiber = 5.4 g Net Carb = 6.6 g
Calories = 504 g Total Fat = 50.3 g Protein = 8.1 g

Chocolate Coconut Brownies

CHOCOLATE FUDGY BROWNIE

Unsweetened Dark Chocolate = 175 g / 1 cup

Unsalted Butter (room temperature) = 113 g / 1/2 cup

Monk fruit = 120 g / 0.6 cup

Whole eggs (room temperature) = 3 large (170 g)

Unsweetened Cocoa powder (sieved) = 30 g / 1/4 cup

Coconut flour = 30 g / 1/4 cup

(OR Almond flour = 120 g / 1 cup)

Salt = 1/2 tsp

COCONUT FILLING

Unsweetened Shredded Coconut Flakes or Desiccated Coconut = 200 g / 2
cups Powdered Sweetener = 20 g / 3 tbsp

Unsalted Melted Butter = 60 ml / 1/4 cup

Whipping or Heavy Cream = 240 ml / 1 cup

CHOCOLATE GANACHE

Whipping Cream = 120 ml / 1/2 cup

Unsweetened Dark Chocolate = 120 g / 3/4 cup

Monk fruit = 50 g / 1/4 cup

DIRECTIONS

1. Preheat the oven at 350F or 180C.

2. Melt the butter and chocolate in a bowl over low heat. Do not overheat the mixture as it can cause the chocolate to split which will result in the fat seeping out from the cocoa butter. Once the mixture is just melted, remove the bowl from heat.

3. Add sweetener and whisk until well combined.

4. Add the eggs, one at a time and whisk until well combined with smooth texture.

5. Add the sieved cocoa powder, salt and whisk until well combined and smooth.

6. Add the coconut flour and fold with a spatula until well combined. The batter should be thick and smooth.

7. Pour the batter into a greased 8 or 9 inch (20 or 23 cm) square pan lined with parchment paper. Spread evenly.

8. Bake for 15 mins. The top should feel a little soft or spongy, but it will firm up once cooled. Do not overbake as the texture will become too dry. Set aside to let it cool.

9. In a bowl, mix all the ingredients for the coconut filling until well combined. Spoon over the baked brownie, spread evenly and set aside.

10. Prepare the chocolate ganache by melting the whipping cream, dark chocolate and sweetener in a bowl or pan over low heat. Once melted, remove bowl or pan from heat and pour over the coconut filling. Spread evenly and sprinkle with flaky salt (optional).

11. Chill in the refrigerator for at least 1 to 2 hours before serving.

12. Cut into 25 x 1 1/2" squares. Clean the knife before each cut.

13. Store in the refrigerator for up to 2 weeks or frozen for up to 3 months.

Total Servings = 25

Nutrition info per serving
Total Carb = 6.9 g Dietary Fiber = 3.1 g Net Carb 3.8 g
Calories = 243 g Total Fat = 22.2 g Protein = 3.4 g

Chocolate Vanilla Marble Cake

Ingredients

DRY INGREDIENTS
Coconut Flour = 90 g / 3/4 cup
(OR Almond flour = 360 g / 3 cups)
Baking Powder = 12 g / 3 tsp
Baking Soda = 1/2 tsp (Optional)
Monk fruit = 150 g / 3/4 cup
Unsweetened cocoa powder = 10 g / 2 tbsp
Salt = 2 g / 1/2 tsp

WET INGREDIENTS
Whole Eggs = 4 large (230 g)
Unsalted Melted Butter = 60 ml / 1/4 cup
Whipping Cream = 240 ml / 1 cup
Vanilla Extract = 2 tsp

DIRECTIONS

1. Preheat the oven at 350F or 180C.
2. In a bowl, mix all the dry ingredients (except the cocoa powder) until well combined. To prevent lumps, it's good to sieve the coconut flour. If batter turns out lumpy, just use a handheld mixer to beat until smooth.
3. Add the wet ingredients (except the vanilla extract) and whisk until smooth and thick.
4. Divide the batter into 2 portions i.e. 2/3 and 1/3 portions.
5. Add the cocoa powder into the 1/3 portion and mix until well combined.
6. Add the vanilla extract into the 2/3 portion and mix until well combined.
7. Scoop both batters intermittently into a 7-inch (18 cm) Bundt pan buttered and floured with cocoa powder or coconut flour. You can also use any suitable pans but it's easier to cook if the pans are shallow. I find that using tall pans, the center tends to be curved and undercooked.
8. Swirl the batter around to create a marble effect with a wooden skewer.
9. Bake for about 40 mins or until a wooden skewer comes out clean.
10. Cool completely before slicing.

T. otal Servings = 14

Nutrition info per serving (Coconut flour version)
Total Carb = 2.0 g Dietary Fiber = 0.6 g Net Carb = 1.4 g
Calories = 107 g Total Fat = 10.2 g Protein = 2.3 g

Nutrition info per serving (Almond flour version)
Total Carb = 7.0 g Dietary Fiber = 3.0 g Net Carb = 4.0 g
Calories = 249 g Total Fat = 22.8 g Protein = 7.6 g

Cinnamon Roll Cake

DRY INGREDIENTS

Almond flour = 240 g / 2 cups

Coconut flour = 60 g / 1/2 cup

Other flour options:

1. Almond flour = 480 g / 4 cups

2. Coconut flour = 120 g / 1 cup

Baking powder = 12 g / 3 tsp

Monk fruit = 50 g / 1/4 cup (This is a much-reduced quantity in order to balance the sweetness from the cinnamon and icing glaze. If you are not doing the icing glaze, then you need to increase the sweetness level in the cake.)

Salt = 3/4 tsp

WET INGREDIENTS

Whole Eggs (room temperature) = 4 large (230 g)

Cream Cheese (in brick style) = 120 g / 1/2 cup (softened)

Unsalted Butter = 120 g / 1/2 cup (room temperature)

Whipping Cream = 240 ml / 1 cup

Vanilla Extract = 1 tsp

INGREDIENTS FOR CINNAMON GLAZE

Ground Cinnamon = 12 g / 1 1/2 tbsp (If you prefer a stronger flavor, you can add more ground cinnamon)

Lakanto Golden Sweetener = 67 g / 1/3 cup (OR any keto friendly sweetener. If you add more ground cinnamon, then you need to add more sweetener here.)

Melted Unsalted Butter = 57 g / 4 tbsp

INGREDIENTS FOR ICING GLAZE

Powdered sweetener = 125 g / 1 cup

Water = 1 to 2 tbsp

DIRECTIONS

1. Preheat the oven at 350F or 180C.
2. In a bowl, mix the softened cream cheese with a spatula until creamy. Add the room temperature butter and whisk until smooth and creamy. Then add the eggs, one at at a time and whisk until combined. Finally, add the whipping cream and whisk to combine. Set aside.
3. In a separate bowl, add all the dry ingredients and mix until well combined.
4. Add the wet ingredients into the dry ingredients and whisk until well combined. The batter is thick and smooth. Transfer the batter into a 9x12 inch (23x30 cm) pan lined with parchment paper. Spread evenly. Set aside.
5. To make the cinnamon glaze, mix the ground cinnamon, sweetener, melted butter in a bowl and whisk to combine. Spoon onto the top of the batter then use a wooden skewer to make a marble effect. Bake for 50 to 60 minutes or until a wooden skewer comes out clean. Cool completely.
6. After the cake has cooled, make the icing glaze. Add the water gradually to the powdered sweetener and mix until you get the right consistency. If the mixture is too thick, add more water. If too dilute add more powdered sweetener. Then drizzle onto the top of the cake.

Total Servings = 20

Nutrition info per serving
Total Carb = 3.2 g Dietary Fiber = 1.3 g Net Carb = 1.9 g
Calories = 176 g Total Fat = 16.9 g Protein = 3.5 g

Pure Coconut Cake

Ingredients

DRY INGREDIENTS

Coconut Flour = 90 g / 3/4 cup

Baking Powder = 12 g / 3 tsp

Baking Soda = 4 g / 1 tsp (This makes the cake softer. But you can reduce the amount to 1/4 tsp or 1/2 tsp or omit it if you are sensitive to baking soda taste)

Monk fruit = 70 g / 1/3 cup (Note: This is mildly sweet so if you like it sweeter, you can increase the amount of sweetener. But bear in mind that the coconut ingredients do have some natural sweetness in them).

Salt = 1/2 tsp

Unsweetened Desiccated Coconut (lightly toasted) = 50 g / 1/2 cup (You can also use unsweetened shredded coconut)

Unsweetened Dessicated Coconut (untoasted) = 20 g / 3 1/2 tbsp

WET INGREDIENTS

Whole Eggs (room temperature) = 4 large (230 g)

Coconut Oil = 60 ml / 1/4 cup

Coconut Cream = 240 ml / 1 cup (You can also use coconut milk but make sure that it is of thick consistency, not diluted ones)

Coconut Extract = 1 tsp (optional)

DIRECTIONS

1. Preheat the oven at 340F or 170C.
2. In a bowl, mix all the dry ingredients (except the desiccated coconut) until well combined.
3. Add all the wet ingredients and whisk until smooth. The batter is thick and smooth.
4. Add the desiccated coconut and mix with a spatula until well combined.
5. Transfer the batter into an 8 inch (20 cm) square pan lined with parchment paper. Spread evenly.
6. Top with the untoasted desiccated coconut and press down gently to ensure they stick to the cake.
7. Bake for about 30 mins or until a wooden skewer comes out clean. It is best to bake at the lowest rack to prevent the over browning of desiccated coconut at the top of the cake.
8. Cool for a bit then cut into 16 servings.

Total Servings = 16

Nutrition info per serving
Total Carb = 2.2 g Dietary Fiber = 1.2 g Net Carb = 1.0 g
Calories = 111 g Total Fat = 11.0 g Protein = 2.1 g

Coconut Cake With Vanilla Buttercream

Ingredients

DRY INGREDIENTS
Coconut flour = 60 g / 1/2 cup
(OR Almond flour = 240 g / 2 cups
Baking Powder = 12 g / 3 tsp
Monk fruit = 25 g / 2 tbsp (Note: This small amount is to balance out the sweetness from the frosting. If you are not doing the frosting, you need to increase the sweetener to 50 g / 1/4 cup)
Salt = 1/4 tsp
Unsweetened Desiccated Coconut (Toasted) = 30 g / 5 1/4 tbsp

WET INGREDIENTS

Whole Eggs = 3 large (170 g)

Coconut Cream = 200 ml / 0.8 cup (see note below)

Coconut oil = 60 ml / 1/4 cup

NOTE: You can replace the coconut cream with coconut milk but you may need to reduce the amount slightly according to the consistency of the batter. You can also replace the coconut cream with whipping cream, yogurt or sour cream. As this is a coconut cake, I highly recommend coconut cream for a more intense coconut flavor.

INGREDIENTS FOR COCONUT BUTTERCREAM

Unsalted Butter (softened) = 113 g / 1/4 cup

Powdered Sweetener = 50 g / 1.4 cup

Coconut Cream = 60 ml / 1/4 cup (You can also use coconut milk but you may need to reduce the amount slightly based on the consistency of the cream. Just add gradually until you get the right consistency of the buttercream. However, coconut cream has a slightly more intense flavor.)

Salt = 1/4 tsp

Coconut Extract = 1 tsp (Optional)

DIRECTIONS FOR THE CAKE

1. Preheat the oven to 340 F or 170 C.
2. In a bowl, add all the dry ingredients (except the desiccated coconut) and mix until well combined.
3. Add all the wet ingredients and whisk until well combined.
4. Add the toasted desiccated coconut and mix with a spatula until well combined. When toasting the desiccated coconut, be careful as they can burn easily. It just takes a short time to lightly toast them.
5. Transfer the batter into a greased pan lined with parchment paper at the bottom. I used a 6 inch or 15 cm round pan with a removable bottom. You can also use a springform pan or any suitable pan. This cake is quite small so you can easily increase the recipe.
6. Bake at the middle rack for 40 to 50 mins or until a wooden skewer comes out clean.
7. Meanwhile, prepare the coconut buttercream.

DIRECTIONS FOR THE COCONUT BUTTERCREAM

1. Beat the butter with a handheld mixer until light and fluffy.
2. Then add the powdered sweetener and beat to combine.
3. Add the coconut cream, salt, coconut extract (if using) and beat until well combined.
4. Chill until ready to use.

ASSEMBLE THE CAKE

1. Cool the cake completely.

2. Spread some buttercream evenly on the top and sides of the cake. The frosting does not have to look perfect as this is an easy and rustic style.

3. Use the back of a spoon to create waves at the sides and top of the cake. If you do not want the cake to look visible after creating the waves, then you need to make the layer of cream thicker.

4. Decorate with fresh strawberries half and sprinkle with unsweetened shredded coconut flakes.

Total Servings = 8

Nutrition info per serving (Coconut flour version)
Total Carb = 3,6 g Dietary Fiber = 1.5 g Net Carb = 2.1 g
Calories = 170 g Total Fat = 17 g Protein = 3.0 g

Nutrition info per serving (Almond flour version)
Total Carb = 7.3 g Dietary Fiber = 3.2 g Net Carb = 4.1 g
Calories = 286 g Total Fat = 26.3 g Protein = 7.2 g

Nutrition info per serving (Coconut Buttercream)
Total Carb = 0.4 g Dietary Fiber = 0.2 g Net Carb = 0.2 g
Calories = 119 g Total Fat = 13.3 g Protein = 0.3 g

Coconut Pandan Cake

Ingredients

DRY INGREDIENTS
Coconut Flour = 90 g / 3/4 cup
(OR Almond flour = 360 g / 3 cups
Baking Powder = 12 g / 3 tsp
Baking Soda = 4 g / 1 tsp (optional)
Monk fruit = 100 g / 1/2 cup
Salt = 1/2 tsp

WET INGREDIENTS

Whole Eggs = 5 large (290 g)
Unsalted Melted Butter = 60 ml / 1/4 cup
Coconut Milk or Cream = 120 ml (Do not dilute with water)
Pandan (screw pine leaves) Juice = 120 ml

GARNISHING (OPTIONAL)
Unsweetened coconut flakes = 10 g

DIRECTIONS TO MAKE THE PANDAN (SCREW PINE) JUICE

Fresh Pandan leaves = 130 g

Water = 200 ml

1. Cut pandan leaves into 1 inch length and place into a blender with the water. You can also use a hand held blender.
2. Blend into a fine texture. Remove and squeeze out the juice using a spoon, hands or towel.
3. Strain the juice and set aside.
4. You can also make extra as the juice can be frozen for months

DIRECTIONS

1. Preheat the oven at 350F or 180C.
2. In a bowl, whisk all dry ingredients until well combined. Set aside.
3. In a separate bowl, whisk all the wet ingredient until smooth.
4. Add the dry ingredient into the wet ingredients and whisk until smooth and creamy.
5. Use a spatula to scrape the sides of batter.
6. Transfer batter into a greased 8x4 inch (20x10 cm) loaf pan (line parchment paper at the bottom).
7. Top with unsweetened coconut flakes.
8. Bake for 40 to 50 mins or until a wooden skewer comes out clean.
9. Cool completely.
10. As an option, you can add more coconut flakes on top of cake for a color contrast.

Total Servings = 16

Nutrition info per serving
Total Carb = 1.0 g Dietary Fiber = 0.5 g Net Carb = 0.5 g
Calories = 67 g Total Fat = 6.3 g Protein = 2.0 g

Coffee Butter Cake - Almond & Coconut
(Short Cut Version)

Ingredients

DRY INGREDIENTS
Almond flour = 150 g / 1 1/4 cup
Coconut flour = 40 g / 5 3/4 tbsp
Baking Powder = 12 g / 3 tsp
Monk fruit = 100 g / 1/2 cup
Salt = 1/2 to 3/4 tsp

WET INGREDIENTS
Unsalted Melted Butter (room temperature) = 225 g / 1 cup
Whole eggs (room temperature) = 4 large (230 g)

COFFEE MIXTURE

Instant Coffee Powder = 25 g / 5 tbsp (For a stronger flavor, you can add up to 30 g but the cake will be more bitter)

Hot Water = 15 ml / 1 tbsp

(Note: Mix together and stir until dissolved then set aside)

DIRECTIONS

1. Preheat the oven at 340 F or 170 C.

2. In a bowl, add all the dry ingredients and mix until well combined.

3. Then add all the wet ingredients including the coffee mixture. Whisk until well combined. The batter is thick and smooth.

4. Transfer the batter into an 8 inch (20 cm) square pan lined with parchment paper. Tap the pan a few times. Of course, you can also use any suitable pan. However, the baking time will depend on what type of pan you use and how thick is the batter. Always test with a wooden skewer for doneness.

5. As an option, top with pecans.

6. Bake for 40 to 45 minutes. I like to use this square pan as it bakes faster. After 15 minutes, I cover with a foil for 15 minutes then remove the foil for the last 15 minutes.

7. Once ready, cool for a while before slicing. I cut the cake into 16 servings, but you can choose to cut them bigger or smaller.

Total Servings = 16

Nutrition info per serving

Total Carb = 2.0 g Dietary Fiber = 0.8 g Net Carb = 1.2 g

Calories = 156 g Total Fat = 15.5 g Protein = 2.9 g

Coffee Cake

DRY INGREDIENTS

Coconut flour = 60 g / 1/2 cup

(OR Almond flour = 240 g / 2 cups

Baking Powder = 8 g / 2 tsp

Monk fruit = 70 g / 5 tbsp (If you are topping the cake with the coffee buttercream, the sweetener should be reduced to around 40 to 50 g in order to balance with the sweetness from the buttercream)

A pinch of salt

WET INGREDIENTS

Whipping Cream = 160 ml / 2/3 cup

Whole Eggs = 3 large (170 g)

Unsalted Melted Butter = 60 ml / 1/4 cup

COFFEE MIXTURE

Instant Coffee Powder = 20 g / 4 tbsp (This amount creates a moderate coffee flavor. If you prefer a stronger coffee flavor, you can add another 1 to 2 tbsp but bear in mind that the taste will be more bitter so you may need to increase the sweetener).

Hot Water = 30 ml / 2 tbsp

(Note: Dissolve the instant coffee powder with hot water then set aside)

DIRECTIONS

1. Preheat the oven at 340 F or 170 C.
2. In a bowl, add all the wet ingredients and whisk until well combined. Set aside.
3. In another bowl, add all the dry ingredients and mix until well combined.
4. Add the wet into the dry ingredients and whisk until well combined.
5. Add the coffee mixture and whisk until well combined. The batter is smooth and moderately thick.
6. Transfer the batter in a greased pan lined with parchment paper at the bottom. I used a 6 inch or 15 cm round pan with a removable bottom. You can also use a springform pan or any suitable pan. This cake is quite small so you can easily increase the recipe.
7. Bake at the middle rack for 30 to 40 mins or until a wooden skewer comes out clean.
8. Cool completely on a wire rack.
9. Dust with powdered sweetener (optional).

Total Servings = 8

Nutrition info per serving (Coconut flour version)
Total Carb = 1.2 g Dietary Fiber = 0.4 g Net Carb = 0.8 g
Calories = 90 g Total Fat = 8.6 g Protein = 2.3 g

Nutrition info per serving (Almond flour version)
Total Carb = 4.9 g Dietary Fiber = 2.2 g Net Carb = 2.7 g
Calories = 206 g Total Fat = 18.0 g Protein = 6.4 g

Coffee Marble Cake

Keto Coffee Marble Cake

Ingredients

DRY INGREDIENTS
Coconut Flour = 90 g / 3/4 cup
(OR Almond flour at 360 g / 3 cups)
Baking Powder = 12 g / 3 tsp
Baking Soda = 1/2 tsp (Optional)
Monk fruit = 150 g / 3/4 cup (Note: You can reduce to between 100 to 120 g for a milder sweetness level)

WET INGREDIENTS
Whole Eggs = 5 large (290 g)
Unsalted Melted Butter = 60 ml / 1/4 cup
Whipping Cream = 240 ml / 1 cup
(Note : As an option, you can add vanilla extract into the original batter)

COFFEE MIXTURE
Instant Coffee = 10 g / 2 tbsp (Note: For a milder flavor, you can reduce to 1 tbsp) Coffee Flavor = 2 tsp (Optional)
Hot Water = 3 tbsp
(Note: Mix together in a bowl, stir to dissolve and set aside)

DIRECTIONS

1. Preheat the oven at 350F or 180C.

2. In a bowl, mix all the dry ingredients until well combined. To prevent lumps, it's good to sieve the coconut flour. If batter turns out lumpy, just use a handheld mixer to beat until smooth.

3. Add the wet ingredients and whisk until smooth and thick.

4. Divide the batter into 2 portions i.e. 2/3 and 1/3 portions.

5. Add the coffee mixture into the 1/3 portion and mix until well combined.

6. Scoop both batters intermittently into a 7 inch (18 cm) square pan lined with parchment paper. You can also use a rectangle or round pan and it's easier to cook with a shallow pan. Try to avoid using any small loaf pan as the higher the batter, the longer it takes to cook and the top will tend to burn so you have to cover with foil. Paper cups or muffin tins are doable too.

7. Swirl the batter around to create a marble effect with a wooden skewer.

8. Bake for about 30 to 35 mins or until a wooden skewer comes out clean.

9. Cool completely then cut into 25 x 1 inch squares.

Total Servings = 25

Nutrition info per serving (Coconut flour version)
Total Carb = 0.9 g Dietary Fiber = 0.2 g Net Carb = 0.7 g
Calories =` 60 g Total Fat = 5.8 g Protein = 1.4 g

Nutrition info per serving (Almond flour version)
Total Carb = 3.6 g Dietary Fiber = 1.5 g Net Carb = 2.1 g
Calories = 139 g Total Fat = 12.9 g Protein = 4.4 g

Cream Cheese Chocolate Cake

Ingredients

FOR CREAM CHEESE BATTER
Cream cheese (softened) = 180 g / 1 1/2 cup
Powdered sweetener = 24 g / 1/4 cup
Egg yolks = 2 large (room temp)
Coconut flour = 10 g / 1 tbsp
(OR Almond flour = 20 g / 2 tbsp)

FOR CHOCOLATE BATTER
Coconut flour = 60 g / 1/2 cup
(OR Almond flour = 240 g / 2 cups)
Unsalted Butter (room temperature) = 160 g / 2/3 cup
Monk fruit = 60 to 100 g / 1/4 to 1/2 cup
Whole eggs (room temperature) = 4 large (230 g)
Cocoa powder (unsweetened) = 30 g / 4 tbsp
Baking powder = 8 g / 2 tsp
Whipping cream = 160 ml / 0.7 cup

DIRECTIONS

1. Preheat the oven at 350F or 180C.

2. In a bowl, mix the cream cheese and powdered sweetener with a spatula until well combined. Add egg yolks and mix until combined. Finally, add the coconut flour and mix until well combined. Set aside.

3. In another bowl, whisk the butter and sweetener until fluffy and the butter has turned into a pale color. You can opt to use a handheld mixer to do this too.

4. Add the eggs one a time and whisk until well combined.

5. Sieve the coconut flour, cocoa powder and baking powder into the batter. Fold to combine.

6. Add the whipping cream and fold until a thick and smooth consistency.

7. Spoon half the chocolate batter into an 8x4 inch (20x10 cm) loaf pan lined with parchment paper. Spread evenly with a spoon or spatula.

8. Spoon half the cream cheese batter on top of the chocolate layer at the middle section only. Spread slightly but do not spread until the sides.

9. Cover with the balance of the chocolate batter and spread evenly.

10. Top with the balance of the cream cheese batter just at the middle only. Then use a wooden skewer to create patterns.

11. Bake at the middle rack for 40 to 50 minutes or until a wooden skewer comes out clean. If the top is browning too fast, cover with foil. I made a mistake by not covering the top; hence the cake was a little burnt at the sides.

12. Let the cake cool completely before slicing.

Total Servings = 15

Nutrition info per serving
Total Carb = 2.2 g Dietary Fiber = 0.9 g Net Carb = 1.3 g
Calories =' 178 g Total Fat = 18 g Protein = 3.6 g

Cream Cheese Coffee Cake

Ingredients

FOR CREAM CHEESE BATTER

Cream cheese (softened) = 180 g / 3/4 cup

Powdered sweetener = 24 g / 1/4 cup (You can also use granulated sweetener)

Egg yolks = 2 large (room temp)

Coconut flour = 10 g / 1 tbsp

(OR Almond flour = 20 g / 2 tbsp)

FOR COFFEE BATTER

Coconut flour = 90 g / 3/4 cup

(OR Almond flour = 300 g / 2 1/2 cups)

Unsalted Butter (room temperature) = 160 g / 2/3 cup

Monk fruit = 100 g / 1/2 cup

Whole eggs (room temperature) = 4 large (230 g)

Baking powder = 8 g / 2 tsp

Whipping cream = 120 ml / 1/2 cup

Instant coffee powder = 20 g / 4 tbsp (The coffee flavor is moderate so if you wish to have a stronger flavor, you can add more instant coffee powder)

Hot water = 15 ml or 1 tbsp

DIRECTIONS

1. Preheat the oven at340F or 170C.

2. Mix the instant coffee powder with hot water and stir to dissolve. Set aside

3. In a bowl, mix the cream cheese until creamy. Then add powdered sweetener and mix until well combined. Add egg yolks and mix until well combined. Finally, add the coconut flour and mix until well combined. Set aside.

4. In another bowl, whisk the butter and sweetener until fluffy and the butter has turned into a pale color.

5. Add eggs one a time and whisk until well combined.

6. Sieve the coconut flour and baking powder into the batter. Fold to combine.

7. Add the whipping cream and fold until well combined.

DIRECTIONS

8. Lastly, add the coffee mixture and fold until well combined. The batter is smooth and thick.

9. Spoon half the coffee batter into an 8x4 inch (20x10 cm) loaf pan lined with parchment paper. Spread evenly with a spoon or spatula.

10. Spoon half the cream cheese batter on top of the coffee batter at the middle section only. Spread slightly but do not spread until the sides.

11. Cover with the balance of the chocolate batter and spread evenly.

12. Top with the balance of the cream cheese batter just at the middle only. Spread slightly then use a wooden skewer to create patterns.

13. Bake at the middle rack for 40 to 50 minutes or until a wooden skewer comes out clean. If the top is browning too fast, cover with foil. The cake tends to be browner at the edges but it's fine.

14. Let the cake cool completely before slicing. Clean the knife after each cut so that it doesn't smudge the cake

Total Servings = 15

Nutrition info per serving
Total Carb = 1.2 g Dietary Fiber = 0.3 g Net Carb = 0.9 g
Calories =` 171 g Total Fat = 17.1 g Protein = 3 g

Cream Cheese Matcha Chocolate Muffins

Ingredients

CAKE BATTER
Coconut Flour = 60 g / 1/2 cup
(OR Almond Flour = 240 g / 2 cups)
Unsalted Butter (softened) = 160 g / 2/3 cup
Whole Eggs (room temperature) = 4 large (230 g)
Monk fruit = 80 g / 1/3 cup
Unsweetened Cocoa Powder = 30 g / 4 tbsp
Baking Powder = 8 g / 2 tsp
Whipping Cream = 160 ml / 2/3 cup

CREAM CHEESE FILLING
Cream Cheese (room temperature) = 230 g / 1 cup
Powdered sweetener = 30 g / 4 tbsp
Egg yolks = 3
Coconut flour = 10 g / 1 tbsp
(OR Almond Flour = 20 g / 2 tbsp)
Uji Matcha Green Tea Powder = 4 g / 1 tsp

DIRECTIONS FOR CAKE BATTER

1. Preheat the oven at 320F or 160C.
2. In a bowl, add the softened butter and sweetener. Whisk until creamy and pale in color.
3. Add the eggs one at a time and whisk to combine.
4. Sieve the coconut flour, cocoa powder, baking powder and salt into the butter and egg mixture. Mix until well combined.
5. Add the whipping cream and mix until smooth and thick.
6. Spoon the batter into greased regular muffin tins or large firm paper cups. This recipe makes 16 muffins using regular muffin tins or 10 muffins using large firm paper cups. Set aside.

DIRECTIONS FOR CHEESE FILLINGS

1. In a bowl, add the cream cheese and sieved powdered sweetener. Mix to combine.
2. Add the egg yolks and mix to combine.
3. Lastly, add the sieved coconut flour and mix until well combined.
4. Divide the fillings into 2 equal portions.
5. Add the uji matcha green tea powder into one of the portions and mix until well combined.
6. Place the fillings into piping bags, cut off the tip and pipe into the middle of the batter. I made 3 versions i.e. cream cheese, matcha green tea and a combo of both fillings. But you can of course, do according to your preference.
7. Bake at the middle rack for about 15 to 20 mins or until a wooden skewer comes out clean.

Total Servings = 16

Nutrition info per serving (Coconut flour version)
Total Carb = 4.8 g Dietary Fiber = 2.2 g Net Carb = 2.6 g
Calories =` 195 g Total Fat = 18.5 g Protein = 4.3 g

Nutrition info per serving (Almond flour version)
Total Carb = 5.6 g Dietary Fiber = 2.4 g Net Carb = 3.2 g
Calories = 271 g Total Fat = 26.1 g Protein = 7.2 g

Cream Cheese Muffins

Ingredients

CAKE BATTER
Cream Cheese (softened) = 80 g / 2/3 cup
Unsalted Butter (softened) = 120 g / 1/2 cup
Coconut flour = 60 g / 1/2 cup
Monk fruit = 80 g / 0.4 cup
Whole eggs (room temp) = 4 large (230 g)
Whipping Cream = 120 ml / 1/2 cup
Baking powder = 4 g / 1 tsp

CREAM CHEESE FILLING
Cream cheese (softened) = 200 g / 1 2/3 cup
Powdered Sweetener = 24 g / 3 tbsp
Egg Yolks (room temp) = 2 large

DIRECTIONS

1. Preheat the oven at 340F or 170C

2. In a bowl, whisk the butter, cream cheese and sweetener until well combined and butter has turned into a pale color.

3. Add the eggs one at a time and whisk until well combined.

4. Sieve the coconut flour and baking powder into the mixture and mix until the batter is smooth. Then add the whipping cream and mix until well combined.

5. Spoon the batter into muffin cups or molds. This recipe makes 8 medium sized muffins in cups and 12 muffins in molds. Fill each cup or mold until 1/2 to 3/4 high. Set aside.

6. Prepare the cream cheese filling by mixing the cream cheese and powdered sweetener with a spatula until smooth. Then add the egg yolks and mix until well combined.

7. Spoon the cream cheese filling into a piping bag, tighten the bag and cut out the tip of the bag.

8. Squeeze the filling into the middle of the cake batter until all the filling is used up.

9. Bake at the middle rack for 15 to 20 mins or until browned and cooked.

Total Servings = 8

Nutrition info per serving
Total Carb = 2.2 g Dietary Fiber = 0.4 g Net Carb = 1.8 g
Calories = 318 g Total Fat = 32 g Protein = 6.7 g

Earl Grey Cake

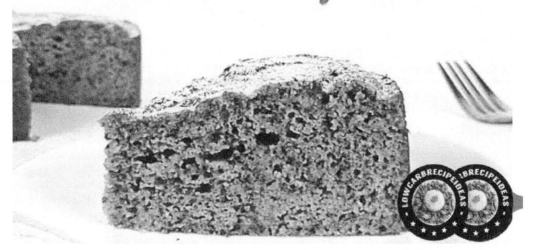

Ingredients

EARL GREY TEA

I used Dilmah Earl Grey Tea which comes in a box of 20 bags with 40 g net weight or 1.41 oz. Hence, 1 tea bag = 2 g

Earl Grey Tea = 3 bags

Boiling Water = 50 ml / 10 tsp

(Note: Cut off the labels and put the bags into a cup. Add the boiling water, cover and steep for 3 to 5 minutes. Then measure out 30 ml / 6 tsp of the steeped tea. Set aside.

DRY INGREDIENTS

Coconut flour = 60 g / 1/2 cup

(OR Almond flour = 240 g / 2 cups)

Baking Powder = 8 g / 2 tsp

Monk fruit = 70 g / 1/3 cup

A pinch of salt

Earl Grey Tea Powder = 1 to 2 bags (Remove the powder from the tea bags. I used 1 1/2 bags of the powder and the flavor is just nice. But if you prefer it stronger, you can add up to 2 tea bags of powder)

WET INGREDIENTS

Whipping Cream = 160 ml / 2/3 cup

Whole Eggs = 3 large (170 g)

Coconut oil = 60 ml / 1/4 cup

Earl Grey Tea = 30 ml / 6 tsp

DIRECTIONS

1. Preheat the oven to 340 F or 170 C.
2. In a bowl, add all the wet ingredients and whisk until well combined. Set aside.
3. In another bowl, add all the dry ingredients and mix until well combined.
4. Add the wet into the dry ingredients and whisk until the batter is thick and smooth.
6. Transfer the batter into a greased pan lined with parchment paper at the bottom. I used a 6 inch or 15 cm round pan with a removable bottom. You can also use a springform pan or any suitable pan. This cake is quite small so you can easily increase the recipe.
7. Bake at the middle rack for 40 mins or until a wooden skewer comes out clean.
8. Cool completely on a wire rack.
9. Dust with powdered sweetener (optional).

Total Servings = 8

Nutrition info per serving (Coconut flour version)
Total Carb = 1.9 g Dietary Fiber = 0.4 g Net Carb = 1.5 g
Calories = 148 g Total Fat = 15 g Protein = 2.7 g

Nutrition info per serving (Almond flour version)
Total Carb = 4.4 g Dietary Fiber = 1.6 g Net Carb = 2.8 g
Calories = 225 g Total Fat = 21.9g Protein = 5.6 g

Flourless Fudgy Brownie
(With Eggless Option)

Ingredients

Unsweetened Dark Chocolate = 175 g / 1 cup

Unsalted Butter (room temp) = 113 g / 1/2 cup

(OR Coconut Oil = 60 g / 1/4 cup for dairy free version)

Monk fruit = 100 to 120 g (1/2 cup)

Whole Eggs (room temperature) = 3 large (170 g)

(OR 3 Flax Eggs for eggless version. Mix 3 tbsp of flaxseed meal with 9 tbsp of water. Rest for 15 mins to thicken)

Unsweetened cocoa powder (sieved) = 30 g / 1/4 cup

Salt = 4 g / 1 tsp

DIRECTIONS

1. Preheat the oven at 350F or 180C.

2. Melt the butter or coconut oil with dark chocolate in a bowl over low heat. Do not overheat the mixture as it can cause the chocolate to split which will result in the fat seeping out from the cocoa butter. Once the chocolate is just melted, remove the bowl from heat.

3. Add sweetener and whisk until well combined.

4. Add the eggs, one at a time and whisk until combined and smooth. For flax eggs, add all at once. The texture will be drier and coarser but it is normal.

5. Add the sieved cocoa powder, salt and fold until well combined and smooth. For the dairy free and eggless version, the batter will be drier and coarser which is normal and the volume will be slightly lesser.

6. Pour the batter into a 7 or 8 inch (18 or 20 cm) square pan lined with parchment paper. Spread evenly.

7. Top with pecans or walnuts (optional).

8. For the regular version, bake for 15 to 17 mins. The top should feel a bit spongy which means that it is done as it will firm up more after baking. Do not overbake as it will be too dry.

9. For the dairy and egg free version, bake for 20 mins. The top will feel soft but it will be firmer upon cooling. After baking, refrigerate for 30 mins so that the texture will be nice and firm.

10. Cut into 12 servings.

Total Servings = 12

Nutrition info per serving (Regular version)
Total Carb = 5.3 g Dietary Fiber = 2.8 g Net Carb = 2.5 g
Calories = 186 g Total Fat = 16.9 g Protein = 3.9 g

Nutrition info per serving (Dairy free & Eggless version)
Total Carb = 5.8 g Dietary Fiber = 3.3 g Net Carb = 2.5 g
Calories = 150 g Total Fat = 13.0 g Protein = 2.8 g

Fruit Cake

DRY INGREDIENTS

Coconut Flour = 120 g / 1 cup

(OR Almond Flour = 480 g / 4 cups)

Baking Powder = 8 g / 2 tsp

Salt = 1/2 to 1 tsp

Spice Powder ;

All Spice = 4 g / 1 tsp

Cinnamon = 8 g / 1 tbsp

Ginger = 4 g / 1 tsp

(Note: If you like the spices to be stronger, you can increase the amount)

Zest from 1 lemon

Zest from 1 orange

Lakanto Brown Sweetener = 100 g / 1/2 cup (OR any keto friendly sweetener)

WET INGREDIENTS

Whole eggs= 5 large (290 g)

Unsalted Butter (softened) = 225 g / 1 cup

RUM Extract = 13 g / 1 tbsp (Optional)

(Note: If you like the RUM flavor to be stronger, you can increase the amount)

INGREDIENTS FOR DRIED FRUITS & NUTS

Unsweetened dried cranberries = 45 g / 1/3 cup

Fresh Strawberries = 50 g / 1/3 cup

Fresh Blueberries = 55 g / 1/3 cup

Coconut flour = 8 g / 1 tbsp

Pecans = 70 g / 1/2 cup (Chopped and lightly toasted)

Note:

Cut the strawberries into small pieces. Then put on a baking pan with parchment paper together with the blueberries to roast at 270 F or 130 C for about 30 to 40 mins. The strawberries will be ready sooner so you can remove them earlier when done. Prick the blueberries with a fork or knife to let the juices run so that they will dry faster. You can also leave them in the oven after the heat is turned off to let them dry further. Just before using, mix all the dried fruits with the coconut flour in a bowl then set aside. This is to prevent them from sinking to the bottom of the cake.

DIRECTIONS

1. Preheat the oven at 320F or 160C.
2. Whisk the butter and sweetener using a handheld mixer until light and fluffy.
3. Add the eggs, one at a time. Whisk to combine.
4. Add the rum extract (if using) then mix to combine. If you wish to add original Rum or Brandy, you can do so but not more than 100 ml otherwise, the cake will be too moist. By adding this amount, the cake will also be more moist.
5. Add the dry ingredients and whisk to combine.
6. Mix the batter using a spatula until thick and smooth.
7. Add the lemon and orange zest, dried fruits and pecans. Mix to combine.
8. Transfer batter into a 7 inch (18 cm) round removable pan or springform pan lined with parchment paper at the bottom and grease well.
9. Spread batter evenly and decorate with pecans (optional)

DIRECTIONS

10. Bake for 1 hour or until a wooden skewer comes out clean. As the cake is dense with quite a lot of fillings, I baked them at lower heat for a longer period. Because of the fillings, the cake tends to be a little crumbly especially after its freshly baked. It will firm up better the next day as it becomes more moist or after refrigerating. The cake actually taste quite good when chilled.

11. After baking, let the cake rest for 15 mins before removing from the pan.

12. Decorate the cake with strawberries, blueberries and dust with owdered sweetener but this is optional.

Total Servings = 10

Nutrition info per serving (Coconut flour version)
Total Carb = 7.9 g Dietary Fiber = 2.4 g Net Carb = 5.5 g
Calories = 283 g Total Fat = 2.6 g Protein = 4.2 g

Nutrition info per serving (Almond flour version)
Total Carb = 13.8 g Dietary Fiber = 5.2 g Net Carb = 8.6 g
Calories = 467 g Total Fat = 40.9 g Protein = 10.8 g

Fudgy & Cakey Brownies

FUDGY BROWNIES

Unsweetened Dark Chocolate = 175 g / 1 cup

Unsalted Butter (room temperature) = 113 g / 1/2 cup

Monk fruit = 120 g / 0.6 cup (Note: This is moderately sweet so you can go from 100 to 150 g depending on your preference)

Whole eggs (room temperature) = 3 large (170 g)

Unsweetened Cocoa powder = 30 g / 1/4 cup

Salt = 1/2 tsp

Coconut flour = 30 g / 1/4 cup

(OR Almond flour = 120 g / 1 cup)

CAKEY BROWNIES

Unsweetened Dark Chocolate = 80 g / 1/2 cup

Unsalted Butter (room temperature) = 60 g / 1/4 cup

Monkfruit = 120 g / 0.6 cup (Note: This is moderately sweet so you can go from 100 to 150 g depending on your preference)

Whole eggs (room temperature) = 4 large (230 g)

Unsweetened Cocoa powder = 30 g / 1/4 cup

Salt = 1/2 tsp

Coconut flour = 90 g / 3/4 cup

(OR Almond flour = 360 g / 3 cup)

Baking powder = 4 g / 1 tsp

DIRECTIONS

1. Preheat the oven at 350F or 180C.

2. Melt the butter and chocolate in a bowl over low heat. Do not overheat the mixture as it can cause the chocolate to split which will result in the fat seeping out from the cocoa butter. Once the mixture is just melted, remove the bowl from heat.

3. Add sweetener and whisk until well combined.

4. Add the eggs, one at a time and whisk until well combined with smooth.

5. Add the sieved cocoa powder, salt and whisk until well combined and smooth.

6. Add the flour (plus baking powder for cakey version), fold with spatula until well combined. The batter should be thick and smooth. At this point, you can choose to add chocolate chips, nuts etc.

7. Spoon the batter into a greased 8 inch (20 cm) square pan lined with parchment paper. Spread evenly.

8. Bake for 20 to 25 mins. The top should feel a little soft or spongy, but it will firm up once cooled. Do not overbake as the texture will become too dry.

9. Cut into 16 servings.

Total Servings = 16

Nutrition info per serving (Fudgy version)
Total Carb = 4.8 g Dietary Fiber = 2.3 g Net Carb = 2.5 g
Calories = 123 g Total Fat = 12.7 g Protein = 2.7 g

Nutrition info per serving (Cakey version)
Total Carb = 3.2 g Dietary Fiber = 1.6 g Net Carb = 1.6 g
Calories = 75 g Total Fat = 7.2 g Protein = 2.4 g

Fudgy Brownie
(Short Cut Version)

Ingredients

DRY INGREDIENTS
Unsweetened cocoa powder = 75 g /
3/4 cup Almond flour = 60 g / 1/2 cup
(OR Coconut flour = 15 g / 2 tbsp)
Monk fruit = 120 g / 0.6 cup
Salt = 1/2 tsp

WET INGREDIENTS
Melted Unsalted Butter (Room Temperature) = 113 g / 1/2
cup Whole Eggs (Room Temperature) = 4 large (230 g)
Vanilla Extract = 1 tsp

DIRECTIONS

1. Preheat the oven at 350F or 180C.
2. Add all the wet ingredients into a bowl and whisk until well combined. Set aside.
3. Add all the dry ingredients into a bowl and mix until well combined.
4. Add the wet to the dry ingredients and mix until well combined. The batter is smooth and thick.
5. Add the chocolate chips and chopped roasted nuts, if using. Mix until combined.
6. Transfer batter into an 8 inch (20 cm) square pan lined with parchment paper. Spread evenly.
7. Bake at the middle rack for 15 to 20 minutes. I prefer to bake for only 15 minutes as the texture will be fudgier. It is done when the surface feels soft and spongy. Do not overbake as the texture will become dry and cakey.
8. Cool completely.
9. Cut into 9 or 16 servings.

Total Servings = 16

Nutrition info per serving (Almond flour version)
Total Carb = 3.2 g Dietary Fiber = 1.8 g Net Carb = 1.4 g
Calories = 92 g Total Fat = 8.1 g Protein = 2.9 g

Nutrition info per serving (Coconut flour version)
Total Carb = 2.7 g Dietary Fiber =1.6 g Net Carb = 1.1 g
Calories = 78 g Total Fat = 7.5 g Protein = 2.4 g

German Chocolate Cake

DRY INGREDIENTS

Coconut Flour = 90 g / 3/4 cup

(OR Almond Flour = 360 g / 3 cups)

Baking Powder = 12 g / 3 tsp

Monk fruit = 120 g / 0.6 cup

Salt = 4 g / 1 tsp

WET INGREDIENTS

Unsalted Melted Butter = 60 ml / 1/4 cup

Whipping Cream = 150 ml / 0.6 cup

Unsweetened Dark Chocolate = 115 g / 2/3 cup (Melt with 90 ml / 6 tbsp hot water) Whole Eggs = 4 large (230 g)

INGREDIENTS FOR FILLING

Unsweetened Pea / Almond / Coconut Milk = 360 ml / 1 1/2 cup Egg Yolks = 3 large

Unsalted Melted Butter = 115 g / 1/2 cup

Vanilla Extract = 1 tsp (Optional)

Monkfruit = 50 g / 1/4 cup

Unsweetened Shredded or Desiccated Coconut = 200 g / 2 cups

Toasted & Chopped Pecans = 125 g / 1 cup

DIRECTIONS FOR THE CAKE

1. Preheat the oven at 350F or 180C.
2. Melt the chocolate with hot water. If unable to melt the chocolate, just microwave for 20 to 30 seconds. Stir until completely melted then set aside.
3. In a bowl, mix all the dry ingredients until well combined.
4. Add all the wet ingredients and the melted chocolate and whisk until smooth and thick.
5. Divide the batter evenly into 2 x 7 inch (18 cm) greased round pans lined with parchment paper. Spread evenly and tap a few times to release any air bubbles.
6. Bake at the middle rack for 20 to 30 mins until a wooden skewer comes out clean.
7. Cool the cakes on a wire rack.

DIRECTIONS FOR THE FILLING

1. Add all the ingredients (except the shredded coconuts and toasted pecans) into a sauce pan.
2. Cook over medium low heat, stirring constantly until slightly thickened. Remove from heat.
3. Add the unsweetened shredded coconut and toasted chopped pecans and mix until thickened.

ASSEMBLE THE CAKE

1. Spread evenly half the fillings onto the bottom layer of cake.
2. Top with another layer of cake.
3. Spread evenly the balance of fillings onto the top layer of cake.
4. Sprinkle with some chopped and toasted pecans (Optional).

Total Servings = 12

Nutrition info per serving (Coconut flour version)
Total Carb = 11.5 g Dietary Fiber = 5.7 g Net Carb = 5.8 g
Calories = 470 g Total Fat = 45.8 g Protein = 7.3 g

Nutrition info per serving (Almond flour version)
Total Carb = 16.6 g Dietary Fiber = 7.9 g Net Carb = 8.7 g
Calories = 607 g Total Fat = 58 g Protein = 12.4 g

Gingerbread Cake

DRY INGREDIENTS

Coconut flour = 60 g / 1/2 cup

(OR Almond flour = 240 g / 2 cups)

Baking Powder = 8 g / 2 tsp

Keto Brown Sweetener = 50 g / 1/4 cup (OR any keto friendly sweetener)

Salt = 1/4 to 1/2 tsp

Ground Ginger = 5 g / 1 tbsp

Ground Cinnamon = 1/2 tsp

Ground Cloves = 1/4 tsp

Ground Nutmeg = 1/4 tsp

Freshly Grated Ginger = 30 g / 3 tbsp

Hot Water = 60 g / 1/4 cup

WET INGREDIENTS

Whipping Cream = 180 g / 3/4 cup

Whole Eggs = 3 large (170 g)

Coconut oil = 60 g / 1/4 cup

DIRECTIONS

1. Preheat the oven at 340 F or 170 C.

2. Firstly, soak the freshly grated ginger with the hot water for about 10 to 15 minutes. This helps to release its flavor.
3. In a bowl, add all the dry ingredients and mix until well combined.
4. Add all the wet ingredients including the ginger mixture into the dry ingredients and whisk until well combined. The batter is thick because ginger is very fibrous and absorbent. Do not add more liquid as the cake will be too wet.
5. Transfer the batter into a greased pan lined with parchment paper at the bottom. I used a 6 inch or 15 cm round pan with a removable bottom. You can also use a springform pan or any suitable pan. This cake is quite small so you can easily increase the recipe.
6. Bake at the middle rack for 40 to 50 mins or until a wooden skewer comes out clean.
7. Cool completely on a wire rack.
8. Decorate with fresh strawberries and blueberries then dust with powdered sweetener (optional).

GINGER GLAZE
If you wish to make a ginger glaze, just soak some freshly grated ginger with hot water. Drain the ginger juice and reserve the grated ginger. Mix powdered sweetener with a bit of the ginger juice and gradually add more juice until you get the right consistency. If the glaze is too runny, just add more powdered sweetener. Remember that if you are making ginger glaze for the cake, the amount of sweetener for the cake needs to be reduced to balance out the sweetness level..

Total Servings = 8

Nutrition info per serving without toppings (Coconut flour version)
Total Carb = 1.9 g Dietary Fiber = 0.5 g Net Carb = 1.4 g
Calories = 169 g Total Fat = 16.4 g Protein = 2.8 g

Nutrition info per serving without toppings (Almond flour version)
Total Carb = 5.6 g Dietary Fiber = 2.2 g Net Carb = 3.4 g
Calories = 282 g Total Fat = 25.7 g Protein = 6.9 g

Japanese Cheesecake - Original

INGREDIENTS FOR CHEESECAKE

Cream cheese = 225 g / 1 cup

Unsalted Butter = 28 g / 2 tbsp.

Whipping cream = 60 g / 1/4 cup

Shredded cheddar or mozzarella cheese = 60 g / 1/4 cup

Egg Yolks = 4 large

Lemon juice = 1 tbps (Optional)

Lemon zest = 1 tsp (Optional)

INGREDIENTS FOR MERINGUE

Egg Whites = 4 large

Monk fruit = 100 g / 1/2 cup

Cream of tartar = 1/4 tsp (OR 1 tsp lemon juice)

(Note: All ingredients must be at room temperature)

Strawberries and powdered sweetener for garnishing (Optional)

DIRECTIONS

1. Preheat the oven at 250F or 120C.

2. Prepare a pan. I used a 6 inch (15 cm) spring form pan as I like the cake to be tall and I lined the sides of the parchment paper slightly higher than the pan. If you do not have a 6 inch pan, you can also use an 8 or 9 inch (20 or 23 cm) pan except that the cake will not be as tall, or you can increase the recipe accordingly. Grease the pan and parchment paper and wrap the pan with aluminum foil to prevent water from water bath to seep in.

3. Melt the cream cheese, butter, whipping cream and cheese in a bowl over a double boiler over low heat until smooth and creamy.

4. Remove from heat and mix in the egg yolks one at a time followed by the lemon juice and zest if using. Set aside.

5. In a bowl, add the 4 egg whites, cream of tartar and whisk with handheld mixer at high speed until stiff peaks (about 5 mins) and it should look shiny and moist. Gradually add the sweetener while beating the egg whites.

6. Fold in 1/2 the egg whites gently into the cream cheese mixture with a whisk then fold in the other half with a spatula until well combined. This meringue is very important so try not to break it by mixing or stirring as the air will be deflated resulting in the cake unable to rise. Instead fold gently as in scooping up so as to maintain its gentle shape.

7. Transfer batter into the pan and tap it a few times to release visible bubbles.

8. Place the cake pans on a big baking dish and fill with hot water about 1-to-2-inch height depending on the height of your baking dish.

9. Bake at the lowest rack at 250F or 120C for 50 mins then switch to 300F or 150C for 30 mins then finally at 350F or 180C for 5 to 10 mins just to brown the top. But if your cake is brown enough then you do not need to increase the heat for the last 5 to 10 minutes. The cake is done when it feels firm at the top. If the cake feels liquidly then bake it longer. Once done, remove pan from the oven. Remove the water bath, foil and let the cake cool for 10 to 20 mins before removing from pan. Every oven is different so you may need to watch the heat and adjust accordingly.

Total Servings = 8

Nutrition` info per serving
Total Carb = 1.2 g Dietary Fiber = 0 g Net Carb = 1.2 g
Calories = 183 g Total Fat = 17.6 g Protein = 5.7 g

Japanese Cheesecake - Chocolate

INGREDIENTS FOR CHEESECAKE

Cream Cheese = 120 g / 1/2 cup

Whipping Cream = 120 ml / 1/2 cup

Unsalted Butter = 28 g / 2 tbsp.

Egg Yolks = 3 large

Dark Chocolate (Unsweetened or 90 to 99% dark chocolate) = 100 g

A pinch of salt

INGREDIENTS FOR MERINGUE

Egg Whites = 3 large

Monk fruit = 120 g / 0.6 cup

Cream of tartar = 1/4 tsp (OR 1 tsp lemon juice)

(Note: All ingredients must be at room temperature)

Strawberries for garnishing (Optional)

DIRECTIONS

1. Preheat the oven at 250F or 120C

2. Use a 6-inch (15 cm) springform pan or 6 inch pan with removable bottom. Wrap the pan with 2 layers of foil to prevent water (from water bath) from seeping into the pan. Line with parchment or reusable baking paper on the bottom and side of pans. As an option, place the pan into another bigger pan. This helps to reduce heat and make the cake more moist and prevent cracks. Set aside.

3. Heat a sauce pan over low heat. Melt the cream cheese and whipping cream then add chocolate, butter and a pinch of salt. Stir to melt the chocolate until smooth and creamy. Remove the pan from heat then add the 3 egg yolks and quickly whisk until well combined then set aside.

4. In a bowl, beat the 3 egg whites and cream of tartar until soft peaks. Add the sweetener gradually as you beat the egg whites.

5. Pour the chocolate mixture into the meringue and fold gently with a whisk. Do not stir or mix otherwise, the meringue will be affected. When folding, the motion should be like scooping something up. After a while, switch to fold with a spatula until well combined. Transfer the batter into the prepared pan. Place the pan onto a suitable baking dish to create a water bath. Then pour boiling water into the baking dish up to half the height of the pan.

DIRECTIONS

6. Bake at the lowest rack at 250F or 120C for 80 mins then switch to 350F or 180C for 5 to 10 mins. The key is to bake it longer with lower heat then increase the heat for a while just to brown the top. If the heat is too high, the cake will rise rapidly until very tall but will deflate or collapse afterwards. The top will also crack. But baking at this lower heat, the cake will rise slowly until about 1/4 to 1/2 inch and it will not deflate or crack. But sometimes, you may get some tiny cracks which are not too bad. Bear in mind that every oven is different, so you need to be aware of your oven and adjust accordingly. For instance, after baking at 250F or 120C for 45 to 60 mins and you noticed that the cake did not rise at all, then adjust the heat to 300F or 150C for the balance of baking time. You could also bake at 250F or 120C for half the baking time then switch to 300F or 150C for the balance half of baking time. I tried baking at 300F or 150C for 80 mins just to simplify the baking process, but the cake rises too high then collapsed and the top cracked. At any point, if you notice the cake rising rapidly then quickly reduce the heat. To know whether the cake is done, just feel the top. If it feels liquidly then its not done so you can bake it longer. If the top is slightly firm then its done. I know this may sound complicated, but it is just a matter or knowing your oven and understanding the right temperature and duration to bake this delicate cake.

7. Once the cake is done, remove the water bath and foil and let it cool for about 20 mins on the kitchen countertop before removing from the pan. This method is easy as it does not require any resting time in the oven.

8. You can enjoy this cake after it's cooled down and the texture will be light, fluffy and jiggly. After refrigeration, you will notice that the texture is' firmer and drier as the chocolate has hardened but you can let it soften at room temperature. It is so delicious when eaten cold too.

Total Servings = 8

Nutrition info per serving
Total Carb = 5.0 g Dietary Fiber = 1.8 g Net Carb = 3.2 g
Calories = 207 g Total Fat = 21.1 g Protein = 4.9 g

Japanese Cheesecake - Matcha

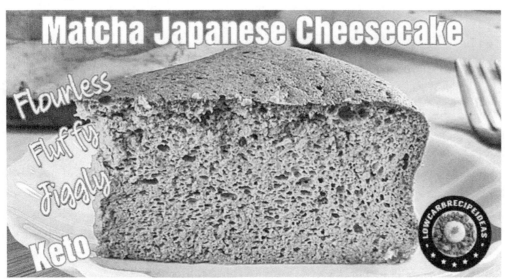

INGREDIENTS FOR CHEESECAKE

Cream Cheese = 300 g / 1.3 cups (I used Philadelphia Cream Cheese)

Unsalted Butter = 28 g / 2 tbsp

Whipping Cream = 60 ml / 1/4 cup

Egg Yolks = 4 large

Matcha Powder (sieved) = 10 g / 5 tsp (It's best to use the culinary grade for baking.
Do not use the ceremonial grade as it is not suitable)

Fresh lemon juice = 1 tbsp (optional)

INGREDIENTS FOR MERINGUE

Egg Whites = 4 large

Monk fruit = 100 g / 1/2 cup

Cream of tartar = 1/4 tsp (OR 1 tsp lemon juice)

(Note: All ingredients must be at room temperature)

DIRECTIONS

1. Preheat the oven at 300F or 150C.

2. In a heat proof bowl, add the cream cheese, butter and whipping cream.

3. Melt over a double boiler at low heat. Whisk until the mixture is smooth and creamy. 4. Remove from heat and add the egg yolks, one at a time. Whisk to combine.

5. Add the lemon juice, if using and whisk to combine.

6. Add the matcha powder and whisk until well combine. Set aside.

DIRECTIONS

7. In another bowl, add the egg whites, cream of tartar and beat at medium to high speed.

8. Add the sweetener gradually around 3 to 4 batches.

9. Beat until stiff peaks.

10. Add half the meringue into the cheese mixture. Fold gently with a whisk. Then add the balance of meringue and fold gently with a spatula until well combined. It's important to "fold" not "stir" to avoid breaking the meringue.

11. I used an 8 inch (20 cm) round pan with a removable bottom. Frankly, I prefer to use smaller pans such as 6 or 7 inch so that the cheesecake will look taller. Unfortunately, this matcha cheesecake does not cook as easily as the original version. I have tried so many times with various baking time combinations and all of them did not work. The cheesecake turned out not properly cooked even though they looked so tall and beautiful. So my last resort was to use an 8 inch (20 cm) pan and bake it at 300F or 150C (same temperature throughout) for 80 to 90 minutes. Thankfully, it worked even with the usual top, bottom heat with fan function.

12. You can also use a springform pan. This time, I used double pans with solid bottom to hold the cake so that I do not have to wrap the pan with foil. If you are not using double pans, then you need to wrap the cake pan with foil to prevent water from seeping inside.

13. Grease the pan and the parchment paper well. Then transfer the batter into the pan.

14. Use a wooden skewer to swirl around the batter to break the big bubbles then tap the pan a few times.

15. Place the cake pan into a bigger pan then fill another bigger pan with hot water until around 1/2 inch high. Then place both the pans into this bigger pan with hot water.

16. Bake at the lowest rack for 80 to 90 minutes.

17. You can open the oven door to feel the top of the cake every now and then to check on doneness. If the top feels firm then it is done. If it feels liquidly, then you need to bake it longer.

18. Once the cake is done, immediately remove the pan and parchment paper and let it cool slightly on a plate. It can be enjoyed warm, room temperature or chilled. I actually prefer it chilled.

19. The che'esecake can be kept in the fridge for up to a week.

Total Servings = 8

Nutrition info per serving
Total Carb = 1.4 g Dietary Fiber = 1.3 g Net Carb = 0.1 g
Calories = 213 g Total Fat = 20.5 g Protein = 7.1 g

Japanese Cheesecake - Zebra

INGREDIENTS FOR CHEESECAKE

Cream cheese = 225 g / 1 cup

Unsalted Butter = 28 g / 2 tbsp.

Whipping cream = 60 g / 1/4 cup

Eggs Yolks = 4 large

INGREDIENTS FOR MERINGUE

Egg Whites = 4 large

Cream of tartar = 1/4 tsp (OR 1 tsp lemon juice)

Monk fruit = 100 g / 1/2 cup

FOR CHOCOLATE BATTER

Unsweetened Cocoa Powder (sieved) = 8 g / 1 tbsp

(Note: All ingredients must be at room temperature)

DIRECTIONS

1. Pre-heat the oven to 250F or 120C.

2. Prepare a pan. I used a 6 inch (15 cm) pan with a removable bottom. You can also use a springform pan. Grease and line the pan with parchment papers. The parchment paper for the side of the pan should be about 2 to 3 inches higher than the pan as the cake will rise quite substantially. But once out of the oven, it will deflate a bit which is normal. If you do not have a 6" pan, you can also use a 7 or 8 inch (18 or 20 cm) pan except that the cake will not be as tall or alternatively, you can increase the recipe accordingly.

3. Melt the cream cheese, butter, whipping cream in a bowl over a double boiler with low heat until smooth and creamy.

4. Remove from the heat and add the egg yolks one at a time, whisking until well combined. Set aside.

5. In a bowl, add the 4 egg whites and beat with a handheld mixer at medium speed. Gradually add the sweetener while beating the egg whites. Once the egg whites reach soft peaks, increase the speed to high and beat until stiff peaks.

6. Add 1/3 of the meringue into the cream cheese mixture and fold to combine. This meringue is very important so try not to break it by mixing or stirring as the air will be deflated resulting in the cake unable to rise. Instead fold gently as in scooping up so as to maintain its gentle shape. Also, do not over fold.

7. Add another 1/3 of the meringue and fold to combine. Lastly, add the balance of meringue and fold to combine.

8. Divide the batter equally into two portions.

9. Add the unsweetened cocoa powder into one of the portions. Sieve it to ensure there's no lumps. Fold gently to combine.

10. To create the zebra stripes, scoop 3 spoons of the original batter into the middle of the pan. Alternate with the chocolate batter. The batter will spread naturally. Repeat this process until all the batter is used up. It doesn't have to be perfect as every zebra cake will look different. This process does require some time and patience. If you do not have the patience, you can just create a marble effect by scooping both batters intermittently into the pan and use a wooden skewer to swirl and create a marble effect.

11. Once the batter is all used up, use a wooden skewer to create a pattern on the top.

12. Tap the pan a few times to release air bubbles.

DIRECTIONS

13. Fill hot water into a suitable bigger pan up to 1/2 inch high.

14. Place an empty pan over the water and place the pan with batter on the empty pan. This method will ensure that no water gets into the batter and also reduces the impact of the heat if the pan with batter sits directly on the hot water. The cake also does not need to rest after baking. This low heat baking will also reduce the chances of the cake cracking and deflate less after baking.

15. Bake at the lowest rack at ; (a) 250F or 120C for 50 mins (This is a slow and steady rise process which is key to prevent rapid rise and fall)) (b) 300F or 150C for 30 mins (This is where most of the rise will happen) (c) 350F or 180C for 5 to 10 mins. (This is to brown the top)

16. The cake is done when it feels firm at the top. If the cake feels liquidly then bake it longer. Once done, remove pan from oven and cool for 15 mins before removing the cake from t'he pan.

17. Every oven is different so you may need to watch the heat and adjust accordingly.

Total Servings = 8

Nutrition info per serving
Total Carb = 1.7 g Dietary Fiber = 0.3 g Net Carb = 1.4 g
Calories = 179 g Total Fat = 17.3 g Protein = 5.3 g

Lemon Blondies

DRY INGREDIENTS

Almond flour = 180 g / 1 1/2 cup

(OR Coconut flour = 45 g / 5 3/4 tbsp)

Monk fruit = 40 g / 3 1/2 tbsp (This is a much-reduced amount in order to balance with the sweetness from the lemon glaze. If you are not doing the glaze, then you need to increase the amount of sweetener accordingly.)

A pinch of salt

Zest from 1 lemon

(Note: There's no leavening agent used here as this is a fudgy or chewy texture. However, if you prefer a slightly cakey texture, you can add 1/2 tsp of baking powder)

WET INGREDIENTS

Whole eggs = 3 large (170 g)

Coconut oil = 60 ml / 1/4 cup

Whipping Cream = 120 ml / 1/2 cup

Fresh lemon juice = 40 ml / 2 3/4 tbsp

INGREDIENTS FOR GLAZE

Powdered sweetener = 125 g / 1 cup

Fresh lemon juice = 30 ml / 2 tbsp

DIRECTIONS FOR THE CAKE

1. Preheat the oven at 340F or 170C.
2. In a bowl, add all the dry ingredients and mix until well combined.
3. Add all the wet ingredients and whisk to combine. The batter is smooth and moderately thick.
4. Transfer batter into an 8 inch (20 cm) square pan lined with parchment paper.
5. Tap the pan a few times to spread the batter evenly.
6. Bake for 20 to 25 minutes or until a toothpick comes out clean.
7. Cool completely on a wire rack.
8. Once completely cooled, make the glaze.

DIRECTIONS FOR THE GLAZE

1. Add the lemon juice gradually into the powdered sweetener. You may not use all of it.
2. Mix until you get a thick paste. However, if you prefer a slightly runnier texture, just add more lemon juice.
3. Spoon the glaze onto the surface then spread evenly.
4. Top with zest from 1 lemon (optional)
5. Trim the edges (optional)
6. Cut into 9 or 12 servings.
7. These blondies can be refrigerated for up to a week. They can be eaten cold or let them come to room temperature before serving.

Total Servings = 9

Nutrition info per serving (Almond flour version)
Total Carb = 2.4 g Dietary Fiber = 1.0 g Net Carb = 1.4 g
Calories = 173 g Total Fat = 16.5 g Protein = 4.0 g

Nutrition info per serving (Coconut flour version)
Total Carb = 0.9 g Dietary Fiber = 0.3 g Net Carb = 0.6 g
Calories = 122 g Total Fat = 12.4 g Protein = 2.2 g

Lemon Blueberry Cake

DRY INGREDIENTS

Coconut Flour 60 g / 1/2 cup

Other flour options;

1. Almond Flour = 240 g / 2 cups

2. Almond Flour = 120 g / 1 cup + 30 g / 1/4 cup Coconut Flour

Baking Powder = 8 g / 2 tsp

Monk fruit = 40 g / 3 1/2 tbsp (This amount is very low so that it balances out with the sweetness from the frosting. If you are omitting the frosting, then you need to increase the sweetener for the batter.)

Salt = 1/8 tsp

Lemon Zest = 1 lemon (1 tbsp)

Fresh blueberries = 150 g /3/4 cup (Mix with 1 tsp of coconut flour so that not all the blueberries will sink to the bottom)

WET INGREDIENTS

Sour Cream = 160 g / 0.653 cup

Coconut Oil = 60 g / 1/2 cup

Eggs = 3 large whole eggs (170 g) OR 6 large egg whites (214 g)

(The batter for egg white option looks a bit dry, but it bakes up fine. The texture is slightly dry, and the cake looks whiter which is a nice contrast for this particular cake. Overall, it still tastes good and is a good alternative for those who have a problem with egg yolks.

Fresh lemon juice = 30 ml / 2 tbsp

Vanilla extract = 1 tsp

INGREDIENTS FOR LEMON BUTTERCREAM FROSTING

Unsalted butter (softened) = 150 g / 2/3 cup

Powdered Sweetener = 120 g / 1 cup

Whipping Cream = 30 ml / 2 tbsp

Salt = 4 g / 1 tsp

Fresh lemon juice = 45 ml / 3 tbsp

DIRECTIONS FOR THE CAKE

1. Preheat the oven at 340 F or 170 C.

2. In a bowl, add all the dry ingredients (except the blueberries) and mix to combine.

3. Add all the wet ingredients and whisk until well combined. The batter is thick and smooth.

4. Add the blueberries into the batter and mix to combine.

5. I used 2 x 6 inch (15 cm) round pans , greased and lined with parchment paper.

6. Divide the batter equally into the 2 pans. Spread evenly.

7. Bake for about 15 to 20 minutes or until a wooden skewer comes out clean.

8. Once ready, remove the cake from pan and cool completely on a wire rack before frosting.

DIRECTIONS FOR THE LEMON BUTTERCREAM FROSTING

1. In a bowl, add the butter and powdered sweetener and whisk until creamy and pale in color.

2. Add the rest of the ingredients and whisk again until smooth and creamy.

3. Chill while waiting for the cake to cook and cool completely.

4. When the cake is ready, spread the frosting evenly on the bottom layer and top of the cake. Spread some of the frosting on the sides too. Then use a cake scraper to smoothen the sides.

5. Decorate with fresh blueberries and lemon slices (Optional).

6. Sprinkle with lemon zest (Optional).

Total Servings = 8

Nutrition Info Per Serving
Total Carb = 4.7 g Dietary Fiber = 0.8 g Net Carb = 3.9 g
Calories = 268 g Total Fat = 26.4 g Protein = 3.1 g

Lemon Blueberry Cake
(Ground Sunflower Seeds)

DRY INGREDIENTS

Ground Sunflower Seeds = 360 g / 3 cups

Baking Powder = 8 g / 2 tsp

Baking Soda = 2 g / 1/2 tsp (Optional)

Monkfruit = 130 g / 2/3 cup

Salt = 4 g / 1 tsp

Lemon Zest = 2 lemons

Fresh or frozen blueberries = 225 g / 1 1/2 cups (If using frozen blueberries, drain off excess liquid before using)

Ground sunflower seeds = 2 tbsp

WET INGREDIENTS

Whole Eggs = 4 large (230 g)

Sour Cream = 80 g / 1/3 cup

Coconut oil = 60 ml / 1/4 cup

Lemon Juice = 45 ml / 3 tbsp

Vanilla Extract = 1 tsp

DIRECTIONS

1. Preheat the oven at 350F or 180C.
2. Mix the blueberries with the 2 tbsp of ground sunflower seeds then set aside. This is to prevent all the blueberries from settling at the bottom of the cake.
3. In a bowl, add the eggs, sweetener and whisk until light in color and thick.
4. Add the sour cream, coconut oil, lemon juice and vanilla extract and whisk to combine.
5. Add the flour, baking powder, baking soda (if using), salt, lemon zest and whisk to combine.
6. Use a spatula to mix until smooth and thick.
7. Grease and line parchment paper on an 8 inch or 20 cm round pan with a removable bottom or spring form pan.
8. Fill half of the batter into the pan then top with half of the blueberries.
9. Top with the balance of the batter, spread evenly then top with the balance of blueberries.
10. Gently press down blueberries until half way.
11. Bake at the middle rack for about 50 minutes or until a wooden skewer comes out clean. The top tends to brown quite quickly so you can cover with a foil midway.
12. Cool the cake for at least 15 mins before removing from the pan.
13. Dust with powdered sweetener (optional).

Total Servings = 12

Nutrition info per serving
Total Carb = 4.9 g Dietary Fiber = 1.4 g Net Carb = 3.5 g
Calories = 141 g Total Fat = 12.4 g Protein = 4.3 g

Lemon Butter Cake
(Short Cut Version)

DRY INGREDIENTS

Almond flour = 150 g / 1 1/4 cup

Coconut flour = 40 g / 5 3/4 tbsp

Baking Powder = 12 g / 3 tsp

Monk fruit = 50 g / 1/4 cup (This is a reduced amount so as to balance out with the sweetness level from the lemon glaze. If you are not doing the glaze, then you need to increase the amount of sweetener for the cake.)

Salt = 1/2 tsp

Zest = 1 lemon

WET INGREDIENTS

Unsalted Melted Butter (room temperature) = 225 g / 1 cup

Whole eggs (room temperature) = 4 large (230 g)

Fresh lemon juice = 30 ml / 2 tbsp (You can use between 20 to 30 ml but do not go beyond 30 ml as the cake may become too soft and crumbly)

LEMON GLAZE

Powdered Sweetener = 100 g / 7/8 cup (If you wish, you can reduce the amount of glaze)

Fresh lemon juice = 30 ml / 2 tbsp (You may not need to use all of it)

126

DIRECTIONS

1. Preheat the oven at 340 F or 170 C.

2. In a bowl, add all the wet ingredients and whisk until well combined. Set aside.

3. In a separate bowl, add all the dry ingredients and mix until well combined.

4. Add the wet into the dry ingredients and whisk until well combined. The batter is thick and smooth.

5. Transfer the batter into an 8x4 inch (20x10 cm) silicone loaf pan or any suitable pan, greased and lined with parchment paper.

6. Spread evenly. As an option, spread the batter to the top of the pan for both short ends. This helps to make the top of the cake flatter so there will be less cracks. Then score a deep cut at the center of the batter. This is to limit the cracks at the middle of the cake. Butter cake has more fats, so it tends to crack more easily with higher heat. However, this is just an option.

7. Bake at the middle rack for 45 to 50 minutes or until a wooden skewer comes out clean.

8. If the top is browning too fast, cover with foil.

9. Once ready, rest the cake upside down for 15 minutes as this will help to prevent the butter from settling at the bottom.

10. Meanwhile, prepare the lemon glaze. Mix the lemon juice gradually with the powdered sweetener until you get the right consistency. If too thick, add more lemon juice. If too diluted, add more powdered sweetener.

11. Once the cake is completely cooled, drizzle the lemon glaze onto the cake. Let the sides drip down naturally for a rustic look. Spread the top evenly then sprinkle with lemon zest.

12. Once the glaze has hardened, you can slice and enjoy.

Total Servings = 16

Nutrition info per serving
Total Carb = 1.6 g Dietary Fiber = 0.8 g Net Carb = 0.8 g
Calories = 156 g Total Fat = 15.5 g Protein = 2.9 g

Lemon Cake
(With lemon buttercream frosting)

DRY INGREDIENTS

Coconut Flour = 90 g / 3/4 cup

(OR Almond Flour = 360 g / 3 cups)

Baking Powder = 8 g / 2 tsp

Baking Soda = 2 g / 1/2 tsp (optional)

Monk fruit = 40 g (This amount is very low so that it balances out with the sweetness from the frosting. If you are omitting the frosting, then you need to increase the sweetener for the batter from 80 to 100 g)

Salt = 1/2 to 1 tsp

Lemon Zest = 1 1/2 tbsp (NOTE : Reserve 1 tbsp lemon zest for topping)

WET INGREDIENTS

Unsalted Melted Butter = 100 g / 8 tbsp

Whole Eggs = 5 large (290 g)

Fresh lemon juice = 90 ml / 6 tbsp

Whipping Cream = 140 ml / 9 1/2 tbsp

INGREDIENTS FOR LEMON BUTTERCREAM FROSTING

Unsalted butter (softened) = 120 g / 1/2 cup

Powdered Sweetener = 90 g / 3/4 cup

Whipping Cream = 30 ml / 2 tbsp

Salt = 4 g / 1 tsp

Fresh lemon juice = 45 ml / 3 tbsp

Lemon zest = 1 tbsp

DIRECTIONS FOR THE CAKE

1. Preheat the oven at 350 F or 180 C.

2. In a bowl, add all the wet ingredients and whisk until well combined.

3. In a separate bowl, add all the dry ingredients and mix until well combined.

4. Add the wet into the dry ingredients and whisk until smooth and thick.

5. Transfer the batter into a greased pan lined with parchment paper. I used a 7 inch (18 cm) square pan.

6. Spread evenly then bake for 30 mins or until a wooden skewer comes out clean.

7. Let the cake cool completely before frosting.

DIRECTIONS FOR THE LEMON BUTTERCREAM FROSTING

1. In a bowl, add the butter and powdered sweetener. Use a handheld mixer to whisk until creamy and pale in color. You can also whisk it manually.

2. Add the rest of the ingredients and whisk again until smooth and creamy.

3. Chill while waiting for the cake to cook and cool completely.

4. Spread the frosting evenly on the top of cake then sprinkle with the lemon zest.

5. Slice the cake into 9 or 12 servings.

Total Servings = 9

Nutrition info per serving (Coconut flour version)

Total Carb = 2.5 g Dietary Fiber = 0.6 g Net Carb = 1.9 g

Calories = 288 g Total Fat = 29.1 g Protein = 4.0 g

Nutrition info per serving (Almond flour version)

Total Carb = 7.4 g Dietary Fiber = 2.9 g Net Carb = 4.5 g

Calories = 442 g Total Fat = 41.6 g Protein = 9.5 g

Lemon Cake With Lemon Curd

DRY INGREDIENTS

Coconut flour = 60 g / 1/2 cup

(OR Almond flour = 240 g / 2 cups

Baking Powder = 8 g / 2 tsp

Monk fruit = 50 g / 1/4 cup

Salt = 1/4 tsp

Zest from 1 lemon

WET INGREDIENTS

Unsweetened Greek or Plain Yogurt = 160 g / 2/3 cup

Whole Eggs = 3 large (170 g)

Coconut Oil = 60 ml / 1/4 cup

Fresh lemon juice = 30 ml / 2 tbsp

INGREDIENTS FOR LEMON CURD

Egg Yolks = 16 large (Note: Using egg yolks makes the texture thicker and more golden in color. But if you prefer the texture to be less thick, you can just reduce the amount of egg yolks and add some whole eggs)

Fresh Lemon Juice = 120 ml / 1/2 cup (About 3 to 4 lemons)

Lemon Zest = 3 lemons

Allulose = 200 g / 1 cup (Note: Allulose is the best option as it does not crystallize when chilled. If you can't get hold of Allulose then you can try Stevia liquid or any other keto friendly sweetener)

Cold Cubed Unsalted Butter = 85 g / 3/8 cup

DIRECTIONS FOR THE CAKE

1. Preheat the oven at 340 F or 170 C.
2. In a bowl, add all the wet ingredients and whisk until well combined. Set aside.
3. In another bowl, add all the dry ingredients and mix until well combined.
4. Add the wet into the dry ingredients and whisk until well combined. The batter is moderately thick and smooth.
5. Transfer the batter into a greased pan lined with parchment paper at the bottom. I used a 6 inch or 15 cm round pan with a removable bottom. You can also use a springform pan. Tap the pan a few times to remove air bubbles and shake it gently to spread evenly. This cake is quite small, but you can easily increase the recipe.
6. Bake at the middle rack for 40 mins or until a wooden skewer comes out clean.
7. Cool completely.
8. Spoon the lemon curd onto the top of the cake and spread evenly. Then spread the sides evenly.
9. Decorate with a lemon slice (optional).

DIRECTONS FOR THE LEMON CURD

1. Add all the ingredients (except the butter) into a saucepan and whisk to combine.
2. Turn on the heat of the stove to low and cook, stirring constantly.
3. Once the mixture thickens and coats the back of the spoon, it is ready.
4. Turn off the heat and remove the pan.
5. Add the cold cubed butter and stir until the butter has melted.
6. Sieve the lemon curd to remove the lemon zest and rough lumps.
7. Store in clean and dry jars in the refrigerator for up to 2 weeks or frozen for months. 8. This lemon curd is rich, thick, mildly sweet and silky-smooth.

Total Servings = 8

Nutrition info per serving (Coconut flour version)
Total Carb = 1.6 g Dietary Fiber = 0.4 g Net Carb = 1.2 g
Calories = 104 g Total Fat = 9.1 g Protein = 4.3 g

Nutrition info per serving (Almond flour version)
Total Carb = 5.3 g Dietary Fiber = 2.1 g Net Carb = 3.2 g
Calories = 220 g Total Fat = 18.4 g Protein = 8.4 g

Lemon Cheesecake
(No Bake)

INGREDIENTS FOR THE CRUST

Almond flour = 120 g / 1 cup

Unsweetened Cocoa Powder = 5 g (2 tsp) (This is optional, but it helps to create a color contrast)

Unsalted Melted Butter = 50 g / 3 1/4 tbsp

Allulose = 20 g / 2 1/2 tbsp (Allulose is recommended as it does not crystallize when chilled. But you can also any keto friendly powdered sweetener if you do not mind the grainy texture)

Salt = 1/4 to 1/2 tsp

INGREDIENTS FOR THE GELATIN MIXTURE

Gelatin Powder = 8 g / 3/4 tbsp

Fresh Lemon Juice = 60 ml / 1/4 cup (This amount makes a stronger lemony taste but if you prefer a milder flavor then you can reduce the lemon juice to 40 g)

INGREDIENTS FOR THE CHEESECAKE

Cream Cheese (softened) = 375 g / 13 oz / 1 3/4 cup (I used Philadelphia Cream Cheese) Whipping Cream (cold) = 225 g / 1 cup

Allulose = 120 g / 1 cup (Allulose is recommended as it does not crystallize when chilled. But you can also any keto friendly powdered sweetener if you do not mind the grainy texture)

Lemon Zest = 2 lemons

DIRECTIONS

1. I used a 6 inch (15 cm) round pan with a removable bottom. You can also use a springform pan. Place the flat side of the removable bottom facing up so that the cake and parchment paper can slide out easily. Line the bottom and sides of the pan with parchment paper. Set aside

2. Mix all the ingredients for the crust in a bowl until a dough is formed. The dough may look crumbly, but it will become a firm dough when you squeeze it. Spread evenly. Use a cup to flatten the dough and a spoon to smooth the edges. Then chill in the fridge until needed.

3. Add the gelatin powder and fresh lemon juice in a bowl, stir to mix then set aside.

4. In a bowl, add the softened cream cheese and mix with a spatula until creamy.

5. Then add the powdered sweetener and mix until well combined, smooth and creamy. 6. Add the cold whipping cream gradually into the batter and whisk until well

combined.

7. Place the bowl of gelatin mixture over a small bowl of hot water. Stir to melt the gelatin. Then remove the bowl of hot water and add 2 to 3 tbsp of the batter into the gelatin mixture. Mix until well combined. Pour the mixture into the batter and mix until combined.

8. Zest the lemons into the batter and mix with a spatula until combined. The batter is smooth and creamy.

9. Transfer the batter into the pan with the crust. Use the back of a spoon to spread evenly.

10. Chill in the fridge for at least 2 hours.

11. Once ready, remove the pan and parchment paper. Smooth the sides of the cake with a frosting spatula.

12. Wipe the knife clean after each cut.

Total Servings = 8

Nutrition info per serving
Total Carb = 3.7 g Dietary Fiber = 1.3 g Net Carb = 2.4 g
Calories = 242 g Total Fat = 22.7 g Protein = 6.7 g

Lemon Cupcakes

DRY INGREDIENTS

Ground Raw Sunflower Seeds = 360 g / 3 cups

Other Flour Options;

1. Coconut Flour = 90 g / 3/4 cup

2. Almond Flour = 360 g / 3 cups

Baking Powder = 8 g / 2 tsp

Baking Soda = 2 g / 1/2 tsp

Monk fruit = 50 g (This amount is low so that it balances out with the sweetness from the frosting. If you are omitting the frosting, then you need to increase the sweetener for the batter between 80 to 100 g.

Salt = 2 g / 1/2 tsp

Lemon Zest = 1 lemon

WET INGREDIENTS

Unsalted Melted Butter = 60 ml / 1/4 cup
Whole Eggs = 4 large (230 g)
Fresh lemon juice = 80 ml / 1/3 cup
Whipping Cream = 120 ml / 1/2 cup

NOTE: For Coconut and Almond flour versions, the whipping cream should be increased to 160 ml. This is because sunflower seeds have higher fat content hence, the amount of liquid needs to be reduced otherwise, the cake is too moist. The rest of the ingredients remains the same.

INGREDIENTS FOR LEMON BUTTERCREAM FROSTING

Unsalted butter (softened) = 120 g / 1/2 cup
Powdered Sweetener = 90 g / 3/4 cup
Whipping Cream = 30 ml / 2 tbsp
Salt = 4 g / 1 tsp
Fresh lemon juice = 45 ml / 3 tbsp
Lemon zest = Zest from 1 lemon

DIRECTIONS FOR THE CAKE

1. Preheat the oven at 350 F or 180 C.
2. In a bowl, add all the wet ingredients and whisk until well combined.
3. In a separate bowl, add all the dry ingredients and mix until well combined.
4. Add the wet into the dry ingredients and whisk until smooth and thick.
5. Transfer the batter into paper cups about 1/2 to 3/4 high. I used big and firm paper cups so I got 10 servings only. If you use small paper cups, you should get more servings around 16 to 18. For coconut flour version, the batter is lesser in volume hence, it will yield a few servings lesser.
6. Bake for about 15 to 20 mins or until a wooden skewer comes out clean.
7. Let the cake cool completely before frosting.

DIRECTIONS FOR THE LEMON BUTTERCREAM FROSTING

1. In a bowl, add the butter and powdered sweetener. Use a handheld mixer to whisk until creamy and pale in color. You can also whisk it manually.
2. Add the rest of the ingredients and whisk again until smooth and creamy.
3. Fill the lemon buttercream into piping bags with suitable piping tips and secure the ends properly.
4. Chill while waiting for the cake to cook and cool completely.
5. Once the cake is completely cooled, frost it. Sprinkle with more lemon zest but this is optional.
6. The frosted cupcakes can be refrigerated for a few days. For freezing, it's better to freeze them without the frosting so that they can be kept for months.

Total Servings = 10

Nutrition info per serving (Gd Sunflower Seed Version)
Total Carb = 4.6 g Dietary Fiber = 1.1 g Net Carb = 3.5 g
Calories = 264 g Total Fat = 26.3 g Protein = 4.9 g

Total Servings = 7

Nutrition info per serving (Coconut flour version)
Total Carb = 4.8 g Dietary Fiber = 0.7 g Net Carb = 4.1 g
Calories = 315 g Total Fat = 31.8 g Protein = 3.7 g

Total Servings = 10

Nutrition info per serving (Almond flour version)
Total Carb = 7.8 g Dietary Fiber = 2.6 g Net Carb = 5.2 g
Calories = 359 g Total Fat = 33.5 g Protein = 7.5 g

Lemon Poppy Seed Cake

DRY INGREDIENTS

Coconut Flour = 60 g / 1/2 cup

(OR Almond flour = 240 g / 2 cups)

Baking Powder = 8 g / 2 tsp

Monk fruit = 30 g / 3 1/2 tbsp (This amount is very low so that it balances out with the sweetness from the frosting. If you are omitting the frosting, then you need to increase the sweetener for the batter to about 60 to 80 g.)

Salt = 1/4 tsp

Lemon Zest = 1 lemon (1 tbsp)

Poppy Seeds = 18 g / 2 tbsp

WET INGREDIENTS

Whipping Cream (room temp) = 160 ml / 0.6 cup

Unsalted Melted Butter (room temp) = 60 ml / 1/4 cup

Whole Eggs (room temp) = 3 large (170 g)

Fresh lemon juice = 30 ml / 2 tbsp

Vanilla extract = 1 tsp

INGREDIENTS FOR LEMON CREAM CHEESE FROSTING

Unsalted butter (softened) = 30 g / 2 tbsp

Cream cheese (softened) = 100 g / 7 tbsp

Powdered Sweetener = 100 g / 0.8 cup

Fresh lemon juice = 30 ml / 2 tbsp

DIRECTIONS FOR THE CAKE

1. Preheat the oven at 340 F or 170 C.

2. In a bowl, add all the dry ingredients and mix to combine.

3. Add all the wet ingredients and whisk until well combined. The batter is quite thick. 4. I used a 6 inch (15 cm) pan greased and lined with parchment paper.

5. Transfer the batter into the pan and spread evenly.

6. Bake for 40 minutes or until a wooden skewer comes out clean.

7. Once ready, remove the cake from pan and cool completely on a wire rack before frosting.

DIRECTIONS FOR THE LEMON CREAM CHEESE FROSTING

1. In a bowl, add the butter, cream cheese and whisk until smooth and creamy.

2. Add the lemon juice and whisk to combine.

3. Add the powdered sweetener and whisk until well combined.

4. If the consistency is too runny or soft, you can add either more cream cheese or powdered sweetener.

5. Chill until ready for use.

6. When the cake is ready, spread the frosting evenly on the top of the cake. You can also frost the sides if you have leftover frosting.

7. Sprinkle with some poppy seeds (Optional).

Total Servings = 8

Nutrition info per serving (Coconut flour version)
Total Carb = 1.5 g Dietary Fiber = 0.6 g Net Carb = 0.9 g
Calories` = 207 g Total Fat = 21.3 g Protein = 1.6 g

Nutrition info per serving (Almond flour version)
Total Carb = 5.2 g Dietary Fiber = 2.4 g Net Carb = 2.8 g
Calories = 323 g Total Fat = 30.7 g Protein = 5.7 g

Marble Butter Cake
(Short Cut Version)

Ingredients

DRY INGREDIENTS
Almond flour = 150 g / 1 1/4 cup
Coconut flour = 40 g / 5 3/4 tbsp
Baking Powder = 12 g / 3 tsp
Monk fruit = 100 g / 1/2 cup
Unsweetened Cocoa Powder = 25 g / 3
tbsp Salt = 1/2 to 1 tsp

WET INGREDIENTS
Unsalted Melted Butter (room temperature) = 225 g / 1 cup
Whole eggs (room temperature) = 4 large (230 g)
Vanilla Extract = 1 tsp
Water = 60 ml / 4 tbsp

DIRECTIONS

1. Preheat the oven at 340 F or 170 C.

2. In a bowl, add all the wet ingredients (except the water) and whisk until well combined. Set aside.

3. In a separate bowl, add all the dry ingredients (except the cocoa powder) and mix until well combined.

4. Add the wet into the dry ingredients and whisk until well combined. The batter is thick and smooth.

5. Divide the batter into 2/3 and 1/3 portions. Add the cocoa powder and water into the 1/3 portion and mix until well combined.

6. I used a 9x5 inch (23x13 cm) loaf pan, greased and lined with parchment paper. This pan is a little big for the recipe (normally I will use an 8x4 inch loaf pan) but the marble effect is well spread and looks more beautiful. But you can use any suitable pan of your choice. You can also increase the recipe for this 9x5 inch pan so that the cake will be taller.

7. Scoop about 2 to 3 spoonfuls of the original batter onto the middle of the pan. Spread it as much as possible. Then alternate with 2 to 3 spoonfuls of the chocolate batter and spread it as much as possible. Repeat the process until the batter is used up. Then tap the pan to spread the batter evenly.

8. You can also choose to use the normal method of scooping the batters onto the pan, alternating the colors then use a wooden skewer to swirl and create the marble effect.

9. Bake at the lower rack for 45 to 50 minutes or until a wooden skewer comes out clean. I found that baking at the lower rack helps to minimize the cracks at the top of the cake.

10. If the top is browning too fast, cover with foil.

11. Once ready, let the cake cool for just a bit before slicing. I actually love to eat the cake a bit warm as it is so soft and fluffy.

12. As an option, you can rest the cake upside down for 15 minutes as this will help to prevent the butter from settling at the bottom. Then turn over and slice accordingly.

Total Servings = 16

Nutrition info per serving
Total Carb = 2.5 g Dietary Fiber = 1.3 g Net Carb = 1.2 g
Calories = 159 g Total Fat = 15.7 g Protein = 3.2 g

Marble Muffins

Ingredients

DRY INGREDIENTS
Almond flour = 360 g / 3 cups
Unsweetened dark chocolate = 100 g / 1/2 cup
Baking powder = 8 g / 2 tsp
Baking soda - 4 g / 1 tsp (optional)
Salt - 4 g / 1 tsp
Monk fruit = 130 g / 2/3 cup

WET INGREDIENTS
Unsweetened Greek or Plain Yogurt = 300 g / 1.2 cups
Unsalted Butter = 100 g / 6 tbsp
Whole Eggs = 6 large (345 g)

Coconut flakes for garnishing (optional)

DIRECTIONS

1. Preheat the oven at 340 F or 170 C.

2. In a small pan, add butter and chocolate. Stir well to ensure that they are melted with low heat until smooth. Set aside.

3. In a big bowl, add all other dry and wet ingredients and mix until well combined. The batter is smooth.

4. Divide the batter into two equal portions.

5. Add the melted chocolate into one of the portions and mix until well combined.

6. Spoon batter into paper cups alternating between the original and chocolate batters.

7. Use a wooden skewer to make a swirl on the batter to create a marble effect.

8. Bake for about 15 to 20 minutes or until a wooden skewer comes out clean.

9. Garnish with unsweetened coconut flakes (optional).

Total Servings = 12

Nutrition info per serving
Total Carb = 8.3 g Dietary Fiber = 3.4 g Net Carb = 4.9 g
Calories = 2`85 g Total Fat = 25.4 g Protein = 9.4 g

Matcha Cake

Ingredients

DRY INGREDIENTS
Coconut flour = 60 g / 1/2 cup
(OR Almond flour = 240 g / 2 cups
Matcha or Green Tea Powder = 12 g / 3 tsp (It's best to use the culinary grade for baking. Do not use the ceremonial grade as it is not suitable) For a stronger flavor, you can increase to 16 g or 4 tsp. The batter may look slightly thicker but it bakes up fine) Baking Powder = 8 g / 2 tsp
Monk fruit 50 g / 1/4 cup
Salt = 1/4 tsp

WET INGREDIENTS
Whipping Cream = 200 ml / 0.8 cup
Whole Eggs = 3 large (170g)
Coconut oil = 60 ml / 1/4 cup

DIRECTIONS

1. Preheat the oven at 340 F or 170 C.

2. In a bowl, sieve the coconut flour, matcha powder and baking powder together. Then add the rest of the dry ingredients and mix until well combined.

3. Add all the wet ingredients and whisk until well combined. The batter is thick and smooth.

4. Transfer the batter into a greased pan lined with parchment paper at the bottom. I used a 6 inch or 15 cm round pan with a removable bottom. You can also use a springform pan or any suitable pan. This cake is quite small so you can easily increase the recipe.

5. Bake at the middle rack for 40 to 50 minutes or until a wooden skewer comes out clean.

6. Cool completely on a wire rack then dust with powdered sweetener and matcha powder (optional).

Total Servings = 8

Nutrition info per serving (Coconut flour version)
Total Carb = 1.5 g Dietary Fiber = 1.9 g Net Carb = 0.4 g
Calories = 171 g Total Fat = 17.1 g Protein = 4.3 g

Nutrition info per serving (Almond flour version)
Total Carb = 5.2 g Dietary Fiber = 3.6 g Net Carb = 1.6 g
Calories = 287 g Total Fat = 26.5 g Protein = 8.4 g

New York Cheesecake

Ingredients

INGREDIENTS FOR THE CRUST
Almond flour = 75 g / 3/4 cup
Unsalted Melted Butter = 45 g / 3 tbsp.
Powdered sweetener = 24 g / 2 tbsp.
(Note: This is a thin crust so if you prefer a thicker crust, you can increase the recipe)

INGREDIENTS FOR THE CHEESECAKE
Cream cheese (softened) = 250 g / 8 oz
Powdered sweetener = 36 g / 3 tbsp.
Sour cream = 120 g / 1/2 cup
Whole Egg = 1 large
Lemon zest = 1 tbsp.
Lemon juice = 1 tsp
Vanilla extract = 2 tsp

INGREDIENTS FOR THE TOPPING (OPTIONAL)

Sour cream = 100 g

Powdered sweetener = 12 g / 1 tbsp.

Lemon juice = 1 tsp

(Note: Mix all ingredients in a bowl to combine then set aside)

DIRECTIONS

1. Preheat the oven at 350F or 180C.
2. For the crust, mix all ingredients in a bowl until a dough is formed. Transfer dough into a greased 6 inch (15 cm) springform pan. Spread and flatten dough evenly. Bake for 15 mins or until browned then set aside to cool.
3. For the cheesecake, beat the cream cheese and powdered sweetener with a handheld or stand mixer at medium speed until fluffy (about 5 mins). Then add the rest of ingredients and beat until well combined. Pour onto the crust and bake for 15 to 20 mins. The center will still be jiggly which is fine. Remove and let it cool until room temperature. Then wrap with foil and refrigerate preferably overnight or at least 5 hours. The longer the cheesecake is chilled, the firmer the texture will be.
4. Once the cheesecake is properly chilled, remove the foil and the side of the spring form pan. If using topping, spread evenly on top of the cheesecake. As an option, you can decorate with berries or serve with berries or any jams.

Total Servings = 8

Nutrition info per serving

Total Carb = 3.4 g Dietary Fiber = 0.7 g Net Carb = 2.7 g

Calories = 254 g Total Fat = 24.8 g Protein = 5.3 g

No-Oven Chocolate Lava Cake

DRY INGREDIENTS

Coconut flour = 60 g / 1/2 cup

(OR Almond flour = 240 g / 2 cups)

Unsweetened cocoa powder = 40 g / 5 tbsp

Baking powder = 16 g / 4 tsp

Salt = 4 g / 1 tsp

Powdered sweetener = 100 g / 1/2 cup

WET INGREDIENTS

Whole Eggs = 4 large (230 g)

Coconut oil = 120 ml / 1/2 cup

Vanilla extract = 2 tsp

Unsweetened Pea or Almond Milk = 240 ml / 1 cup

INGREDIENTS FOR MOLTEN CHOCOLATE

Unsweetened dark chocolate chips or squares = 50 g (I used Baker's unsweetened dark chocolate bars and just cut them up into smaller pieces)

If you prefer more molten chocolate, then just add more chocolate.

FOR STEAMING
1 large pot
480 ml / 2 cups hot water
1 towel

DIRECTIONS

1. In a bowl, add the eggs and powdered sweetener. Whisk until fluffy or foamy. You can use a mixer too.
2. Add the coconut oil, vanilla extract, milk and whisk to combine.
3. Sieve the coconut flour, cocoa powder, baking powder and salt into the wet mixture. Whisk until smooth and thick. Switch to a spatula and mix well. The batter will thicken up further as it sits.
4. Use any suitable teacups or ramekins and brush with coconut oil. If you wish to remove the cake from the cups nicely, then add a layer of sweetener after brushing with oil.
5. Spoon batter into the cups, top with chocolate chips or squares then cover with some batter. I used cups with 120 ml capacity.
6. Place filled cups into a large pot and add the hot water.
7. Cover the pot with a towel then cover with the lid of the pot. Fold back the towel and steam over medium heat for 10 to 12 mins.
8. Enjoy the cake immediately after steaming for that melt in the mouth deliciousness.
9. As an option, you can dust with some powdered sweetener on top of the cake.

Total Servings = 7

Nutrition info per serving
Total Carb = 7.2 g Dietary Fiber = 3.7 g Net Carb = 3.5 g
Calories = 125 g Total Fat = 10.6 g Protein = 6.1 g

Peanut Butter Brownie Bars

Keto Peanut Butter Brownie Bars

INGREDIENTS FOR FUDGY BROWNIE LAYER

Unsweetened chocolate = 175 g / 1 cup (Note: I used Baker's
Unsweetened Chocolate, but you can use any suitable chocolate)

Unsalted Butter (room temperature) = 113 g / 1/2 cup

Monk fruit = 120 g / 1/2 cup

Unsweetened Cocoa Powder (sieved) = 30 g / 1/4 cup

Coconut flour = 30 g / 1/4 cup

(Almond flour 120 g / 1 cup)

Whole Eggs (room temperature) = 3 large (170 g)

Salt = 1/2 tsp

INGREDIENTS FOR PEANUT BUTTER LAYER

Unsweetened Creamy Peanut Butter = 300 g / 1 1/4 cup

INGREDIENTS FOR NUTTY CHOCOLATE LAYER

Unsweetened Dark Chocolate = 220 g / 1 1/4 cup (I used Dark Chocolate sweetened with stevia hence, I did not add any sweeteners. If you are using unsweetened dark chocolate, then you may add any sweetener about 50 g / 1/4 cup. Add the sweetener after you remove the pan from the heat. Whisk and adjust taste accordingly.)

Unsalted Butter (room temperature) = 14 g / 1 tbsp

Toasted Nuts (Chopped) = 150 g / 1 cup (I used a combination of almonds and pecans but you can use any nuts of your choice)

Coarse sea salt = A handful

DIRECTIONS

1. Preheat the oven at 350F or 180C.

2. Melt the butter and chocolate in a bowl over the stove at low heat. You can also use the microwave to melt at intervals. Once the chocolate is almost melted, turn off the heat and remove the pan. Just whisk until it is fully melted. Do not overheat the mixture as it can cause the chocolate to split resulting in the fat seeping out from the cocoa butter.

3. Add the sweetener and whisk until combined.

4. Add the eggs one at a time and whisk to combine until the texture is smooth and thick.

5. Add the salt, sieved cocoa powder and whisk until combined.

6. Add the coconut flour and fold with a spatula until well combined. The texture should be smooth and thick.

7. I used 3 small rectangular pans measuring 7x3.5x3 inch (18x9x8 cm) so that it is easier to cut into bars, but you can also use 8 or 9 inch (20 or 23 cm) square pans or any suitable rectangular pans. Line the pans with parchment paper. I divided the batter equally into the 3 pans and spread evenly.

DIRECTIONS

8. Bake for 12 to 15 mins. Do not overbake as it can cause the brownie to be too dry. During baking, the top may bulge up but it is fine as you can use the back of a spoon to flatten it after baking. The top of the brownie may feel spongy after baking but will firm up once cooled.

9. Cool the brownie completely.

10. Once the brownie layer is cooled, top with the peanut butter and spread evenly.

11. Tap the pans to even out the peanut butter.

12. Freeze for 30 minutes and meanwhile, prepare the nutty chocolate layer.

13. Melt the chocolate and butter over low heat. Do not overheat. Remove the pan from heat and whisk in the sweetener, if using.

14. Add the nuts and mix until well combined.

15. Add the nut mixture onto the peanut butter layer and spread evenly.

16. Sprinkle with coarse sea salt.

17. Chill in the refrigerator for a few hours or until set and firm.

18. Cut into bars. If they are not firm enough, just chill them further after cutting.

19. These peanut butter brownie bars can be refrigerated up to 1 week or frozen for up to 3 months.

Total Servings = 18

Nutrition info per serving
Total Carb = 9.7 g Dietary Fiber = 4.5 g Net Carb = 5.2 g
Calories = 229 g Total Fat = 21.8 g Protein = 6 g

Peanut Butter Muffins

Ingredients

DRY INGREDIENTS
Almond flour = 240 g / 2 cups
(OR Coconut flour = 60 g / 1/2 cup)
(OR Almond flour = 120 g / 1 cup + Coconut flour = 30 g / 1/4 cup)
Baking powder = 8 g / 2 tsp
Baking soda = 1/4 to 1/2 tsp (optional)
Salt = 1/2 tsp
Monk fruit = 70 g / 1/3 cup

DRY INGREDIENTS
Whipping cream or yogurt = 200 g / 0.83 cup
Whole eggs = 4 large (230 g)
Unsalted Melted butter = 40 g / 2 3/4 tbsp.
Sugar free chunky or smooth peanut butter = 200 g

DIRECTIONS

1. Preheat the oven at 350F or 180C.
2. In a bowl, add cream, eggs and butter and whisk until well combined.
3. Add peanut butter and whisk until well combined.
4. Add all dry ingredients and mix with a spatula until smooth.
5. Spoon mixture into muffin cups up to 1/2 or 3/4 full to allow space for the muffins to rise.
6. Bake at the middle rack for about 15 to 20 mins or until a wooden skewer comes out clean.

Total Servings = 8

Nutrition info per serving
Total Carb = 3.4 g Dietary Fiber = 0.7 g Net Carb = 2.7 g
Calories = 254 g Total Fat = 24.8 g Protein = 5.3 g

Pumpkin Pie Spice Cake

DRY INGREDIENTS

Coconut flour = 60 g / 1/2 cup

(OR Almond flour = 240 g / 2 cups

Baking Powder = 8 g / 2 tsp

Monk fruit = 24 g / 2 tbsp (Note: This small amount is to balance out the sweetness from the frosting. If you are not doing the frosting, you need to increase the sweetener to 60 g / 5 tbsp.)

Salt = 2 g / 1/2 tsp

Pumpkin Pie Spice Powder ;

Cinnamon = 2 tsp Nutmeg = 1/2 tsp Ginger = 1/2 tsp Cloves = 1/4 tsp

DRY INGREDIENTS

Whipping Cream = 190 ml / 0.8 cup

Whole Eggs = 3 large (170 g)

Coconut oil = 60 ml / 1/4 cup

INGREDIENTS FOR CREAM CHEESE FROSTING

Cream Cheese (softened) = 113 g / 1/2 cup
Unsalted Butter (softened) = 60 g / 1/2 cup
Powdered Sweetener = 50 g / 4 tbsp
Pumpkin Pie Spice Extract = 1 tsp (optional)

DIRECTIONS FOR THE CAKE

1. Preheat the oven at 340 F or 170 C.
2. In a bowl, add all the wet ingredients and whisk until well combined. Set aside.
3. In another bowl, add all the dry ingredients and mix until well combined.
4. Add the wet into the dry ingredients and whisk until the batter is smooth and moderately thick.
5. Transfer the batter into a greased pan lined with parchment paper at the bottom. I used a 6 inch or 15 cm round pan with a removable bottom. You can also use a spring form pan or any suitable pan. This cake is quite small so you can easily increase the recipe.
6. Bake at the middle rack for 40 mins or until a wooden skewer comes out clean.
7. Cool completely on a wire rack.

DIRECTIONS FOR THE CREAM CHEESE FROSTING

1. Use a spatula to mix the cream cheese and butter until creamy.
2. Add the powdered sweetener, pumpkin pie spice extract (if using) and mix until well combined.
3. Chill until ready to use.
4. Once the cake is cooled, spread the frosting evenly on the top of the cake.
5. Dust with some pumpkin pie spice powder.

Total Servings = 8

Nutrition info per serving (Coconut flour version)
Total Carb = 1.9 g Dietary Fiber = 0.4 g Net Carb = 1.5 g
Calories = 159 g Total Fat = 16.1 g Protein = 2.8 g

Nutrition info per serving (Almond flour version)
Total Carb = 5.6 g Dietary Fiber = 2.2 g Net Carb = 3.4 g
Calories = 274 g Total Fat = 25.5 g Protein = 6.9 g

Pure Sesame Seed Cake

Ingredients

DRY INGREDIENTS
Ground Black Sesame Seeds = 120 g / 1 cup
Ground White Sesame Seeds = 120 g / 1 cup
Baking Powder = 12 g / 3 tsp
Monk fruit = 60 g / 1/4 cup.
Salt = 1/4 to 1/2 tsp

WET INGREDIENTS
Whipping Cream = 200 ml / 0.8 cup
Whole Eggs = 3 large (170 g)
Coconut oil = 60 ml / 1/4 cup

IMPORTANT NOTES

1. For both raw black and white sesame seeds, you can easily grind them in a multi grinder, coffee or spice grinder, powerful food processor / blender. Do not overgrind them as they can become a paste or butter.

2. For black sesame seeds, you can also use roasted and pre-ground ones that comes in a tin which are available in supermarkets. Black sesame seeds tend to be nuttier and smokier. They have their hulls (shells) intact and are more flavorful.

3. White sesame seeds have their hulls removed and they have a slightly sweet and nutty flavor. They also taste a little less intense than the black ones.

4. If you prefer a more intense flavor, you can use all black sesame seeds for the cake. Similarly, if you prefer a milder taste, you can use all white sesame seeds. The ratios are the same.

5. There is a mild hint of bitterness in this cake which mostly comes from the black sesame seeds. Hence, if you use all black sesame seeds, the cake may have a little stronger taste of bitterness and the cake will be a lot darker in color. If these are not an issue to you, feel free to use 100% black sesame seeds.

DIRECTIONS

1. Preheat the oven at 340 F or 170 C.

2. In a bowl, add all the dry ingredients and mix until well combined.

3. Add all the wet ingredients and whisk until well combined. The batter is smooth and moderately thick.

4. Transfer the batter into a greased pan lined with parchment paper at the bottom. I used a 6 inch or 15 cm round pan with a removable bottom. You can also use a springform pan or any suitable pan.

5. Bake at the middle rack for 50 to 55 minutes or until a wooden skewer comes out clean. It takes a little longer to bake this cake as it is thicker than my other 6 inch cakes. Of course, if you use a bigger pan, then the cooking time will be shorter.

6. Cool completely on a wire rack then dust with powdered sweetener (optional).

Total Servings = 8

Nutrition` info per serving
Total Carb = 6.1 g Dietary Fiber = 4.5 g Net Carb = 1.6 g
Calories = 346 g Total Fat = 28.9 g Protein = 2.1 g

Raspberry Cream Cheese Cake

DRY INGREDIENTS

Coconut Flour = 120 g / 1 cup

(OR Almond Flour = 480 g / 4 cups)

Baking Powder = 12 g / 3 tsp

Salt = 1/2 to 1 tsp

Monk fruit = 80 / 0.4 cup (This is a reduced amount to balance with the sweetness from the frosting. If you are not doing the frosting, you can increase the amount of sweetener from 100 to 120 g.

Fresh Raspberries = 90 g / 3/4 cup (Plus a few extras for decorating - optional)
Mix the raspberries with 1 tbsp of coconut flour to prevent them from sinking to the bottom of the cake.

WET INGREDIENTS

Unsalted Butter (room temp) = 120 g / 1/2 cup

Cream Cheese (room temp) = 120 g / 1/2 cup

Whole eggs = 3 large (170 g)

Whipping Cream = 240 ml / 1 cup

Vanilla Extract = 3 tsp

INGREDIENTS FOR BUTTERCREAM FROSTING

Unsalted Butter (room temp) = 120 g / 1/2 cup

Powdered Sweetener = 50 g / 1/4 cup

Whipping Cream = 45 ml / 3 tbsp

Salt = 1/2 to 1 tsp

Vanilla Extract = 2 tsp

Fresh lemon juice = 2 to 3 tbsp (Optional)

Zest from 1 lemon (Optional)

DIRECTIONS FOR THE CAKE

1. Preheat the oven at 350F or 180C.
2. In a bowl, add all the dry ingredients and mix until well combined. Set aside.
3. In another bowl, add the butter, cream cheese and sweetener. Use a handheld mixer and beat at medium to high speed until light and fluffy.
4. Add the eggs, one at a time and whisk until combined.
5. Add the vanilla extract and whipping cream and whisk until combined.
6. Add the dry ingredients and whisk until thick and smooth.
7. Grease a 7 inch (18 cm) round pan with removable bottom or spring form pan. Line with parchment paper at the bottom.
8. Divide batter into 3 even portions.
9. Spread 1 portion of the batter at the bottom of the pan and top with half of the raspberries.
10. Spread evenly with another portion of the batter and top with balance of the raspberries.
11. Spread evenly with the balance of the batter.
12. Bake for 50 to 60 mins or until a wooden skewer comes out clean.
13. Let the cake cool for 15 mins before removing from the pan.
14. Let the cake cool completely before decorating it.
15. You can decorate the cake with or without frosting so it is totally up to your preference.

DIRECTIONS FOR THE BUTTERCREAM FROSTING

1. Beat the butter with a handheld mixer until the color turns pale.

2. Then add the powdered sweetener and beat until well combined, smooth and creamy.

3. Add the whipping cream, salt, vanilla extract, lemon juice and zest (if using) and beat until well combined and smooth.

Total Servings = 10

Nutrition info per serving (Coconut flour version without frosting) Total Carb = 3.7 g Dietary Fiber = 1.2 g Net Carb = 2.5 g Calories = 231 g Total Fat = 23.1 g Protein = 3.6 g

Nutrition info per serving (Almond flour version without frosting) Total Carb = 9.6 g Dietary Fiber = 4.1 g Net Carb = 5.5 g Calories = 416 g Total Fat = 38 g Protein = 10.2 g

Red Velvet Cupcakes

DRY INGREDIENTS

Coconut Flour = 90 g / 3/4 cup

(OR Almond Flour = 360 g / 3 cups)

Baking Soda = 4 g / 1 tsp

Monk fruit = 20 g / 1 1/4 tbsp (This small amount of sweetener is to balance out the sweetness from the frosting.)

Salt = 1/2 tsp

Unsweetened Cocoa Powder = 4 g / 1 tsp (Optional)

WET INGREDIENTS

Whole Eggs = 4 large (230 g)

Melted Unsalted Butter = 60 ml / 1/4 cup

Whipping Cream = 240 ml / 1 cup

Vanilla Extract = 2 tsp

White Vinegar = 1 tsp

Red Food Coloring = 6 tsp (Note: The amount may be different depending on the type of food coloring you use so please adjust accordingly.)

INGREDIENTS FOR CREAMCHEESE FROSTING

Unsalted Butter (room temp) = 113 g / 1/2 cup

Cream Cheese (room temp) = 225 g / 8 oz / 1 cup

Vanilla Extract = 1 tsp

Salt = 1/8 tsp

Powdered sweetener = 120 g / 1 cup

DIRECTIONS FOR THE CAKE

1. Preheat the oven at 340F or 170C.
2. In a bowl, mix all the dry ingredients until well combined.
3. Add all the wet ingredients (except the red food coloring) and whisk until well combined. The batter should be smooth and thick.
4. Add the red food coloring and mix until well combined.
5. Spoon the batter into paper cups. I used small but firm paper cups and I got 11 cupcakes out of this recipe. The amount may vary depending on the size of your paper cups. Fill the batter until 3/4 high.
6. Bake for about 15 to 20 mins or until a wooden skewer comes out clean.
7. Let the cupcakes cool completely then only do the frosting.

DIRECTIONS FOR THE CREAMCHEESE FROSTING

1. Beat the butter with a handheld mixer until pale and creamy.
2. Add the cream cheese and beat to combine.
3. Add the vanilla extract, salt and beat to combine.
4. Add the powdered sweetener and beat until well combined. The texture should be creamy and thick.
5. Fill the frosting into piping bags with any piping tips of your choice. Then refrigerate until ready to use.

Total Servings = 11

Nutrition info per serving (Coconut flour version)
Total Carb = 2.2 g Dietary Fiber = 0.5 g Net Carb = 1.7 g
Calories = 277 g Total Fat = 28.3 g Protein = 4.4 g

Nutrition info per serving (Almond flour version)
Total Carb = 6.2 g Dietary Fiber = 2.4 g Net Carb = 3.8 g
Calories = 403 g Total Fat = 38.5 g Protein = 8.9 g

Strawberry Cream Cheese Cupcakes

DRY INGREDIENTS

Coconut Flour = 120 g / 1 cup

(OR Almond Flour = 480 g / 4 cups)

Baking Powder = 12 g / 3 tsp

Salt = 1/2 to 1 tsp

Zest from 1 lemon

Monk fruit = 25 g / 2 tbsp (This is a reduced amount to balance out the sweetness level from the frosting and the strawberry jam. If you are not doing the frosting then you need to increase the sweetener for the cake)

WET INGREDIENTS

Unsalted Butter (softened) = 120 g / 1/2 cup

Cream Cheese (softened) = 120 g / 1/2 cup

Whole Eggs (room temp) = 3 large (170 g)

Whipping Cream = 240 ml / 1 cup

Vanilla Extract = 2 tsp

INGREDIENTS FOR CREAMCHEESE FROSTING & STRAWBERRY JAM

Unsalted Butter (softened) = 100 g / 7 tbsp

Cream Cheese (softened) = 160 g / 11 tbsp

Powdered Sweetener = 120 g / 1 cup

Keto Strawberry Jam = 120 g / 6 tbsp (You can refer to the recipe from my youtube channel)

DIRECTIONS FOR THE CAKE

1. Preheat the oven at 340F or 170C.
2. In a big bowl, add the butter, cream cheese and sweetener. Use a handheld mixer to whisk until light and fluffy.
3. Add the eggs one at a time and whisk to combine.
4. Add the whipping cream and vanilla extract and whisk to combine.
5. Add the coconut flour, baking powder, salt and lemon zest. Whisk until well combined.
6. Use a spatula to scrape the sides and mix well.
7. Spoon the batter into cupcakes. I used big and firm paper cups, so it came out to be 10 servings. If you are using smaller paper cups, then it will yield more cupcakes. If you are using thin paper cups, it's best to place them in muffin tins so that they can be held firmly.
8. Spread the top of batter evenly.
9. Bake for about 15 to 20 mins or until a wooden skewer comes out clean.
10. Let the cupcakes cool completely before frosting.

DIRECTIONS FOR CREAM CHEESE FROSTING AND STRAWBERRY JAM

1. In a bowl, add the butter and cream cheese. Whisk with a handheld mixer until light and fluffy.
2. Add the powdered sweetener and whisk until smooth and creamy.
3. Spoon the cream into a piping bag and secure with a clip. Refrigerate until ready to use.
4. Spoon the strawberry jam into another piping bag and refrigerate until ready to use.
5. As my keto strawberry jam is quite chunky and the blueberries are whole, I put them into a blender and blend until a smooth consistency. This is easier for the piping and to make the marbling effect. As there are blueberries mixed in the jam, after blending, the color of the jam is slightly bluish red instead of bright red.
6. Once the cupcakes are completely cooled, pipe the cream and the jam onto the top of the cake then use a toothpick or wooden skewer to swirl around to create the marble effect.

Total Servings = 10

Nutrition info per serving (Coconut flour version)
Total Carb = 3.1 g Dietary Fiber = 0.6 g Net Carb = 2.5 g
Calories = 354 g Total Fat = 36.7 g Protein = 4.7 g

Nutrition info per serving (Almond flour version)
Total Carb = 9.0 g Dietary Fiber = 3.5 g Net Carb = 5.5 g
Calories = 539 g Total Fat = 51.6 g Protein = 11.4 g

Strawberry Yogurt Cupcakes

DRY INGREDIENTS

Coconut flour = 90 g / 3/4 cup

(OR Almond flour = 360 g / 3 cups)

Baking Powder = 8 g / 2 tsp

Monk fruit = 70 g / 1/3 cup

Salt = 1/2 tsp

Fresh Strawberries (cubed) = 200 g / 1 cup

Coconut Flour = 14 g / 2 tbsp

(Note: Mix to combine then set aside. This is to prevent all the strawberries from settling at the bottom)

WET INGREDIENTS

Unsweetened Greek or Plain Yogurt = 240 g / 1 cup

Whole Eggs = 4 large (230 g)

Coconut Oil = 60 ml / 1/4 cup

Vanilla Extract = 2 tsp

DIRECTIONS

1. Preheat the oven at 340F or 170C.

2. In a bowl, whisk all the wet ingredients until well combined then set aside.

3. In another bowl, mix all the dry ingredients until well combined.

4. Add the wet into the dry ingredients and whisk until well combined. Lastly, add the cubed strawberries and mix to combine.

5. The batter is thick but it will bake up to a soft and moist cake.

6. Spoon the batter into paper cups until 3/4 height. Spread evenly. This recipe makes about 12 small cupcakes.

7. Bake for 15 to 20 minutes or until a toothpick comes out clean.

8. Cool completely.

9. Decorate with mini strawberries then dust with powdered sweetener (optional).

Total Servings = 12

Nutrition info per serving (Coconut flour version)
Total Carb = 2.0 g Dietary Fiber = 0.9 g Net Carb = 1.1 g
Calories = 83 g Total Fat = 6.3 g Protein = 4.0 g

Nutrition info per serving (Almond flour version)
Total Carb = 5.7 g Dietary Fiber = 2.7 g Net Carb = 3.0 g
Calories = 198 g Total Fat = 15.6 g Protein = 8.2 g

Taiwanese Chocolate Castella Cake

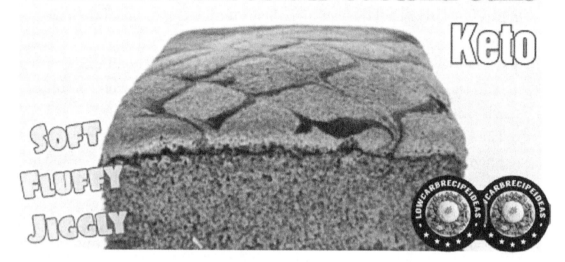

INGREDIENTS FOR CHOCOLATE MIXTURE

Coconut Flour = 30 g / 1/4 cup

(OR Almond flour = 120 g / 1 cup. Using almond flour will yield a slightly bigger volume)

Unsweetened Cocoa Powder = 25 g / 4 tbsp

Eggs Yolks (room temperature) = 5 large

Coconut Oil = 50 ml / 4 tbsp

Unsweetened Milk = 80 ml / 6 tbsp (I used Pea Milk but you can also use almond milk or any keto friendly milk)

Vanilla Extract = 1 tsp (Optional)

INGREDIENTS FOR THE MERINGUE

Egg Whites (room temperature) = 5 large (175 g)

Monk fruit = 100 g / 1/2 cup

Salt = 1/4 tsp

INGREDIENTS FOR LEAF DESIGN AT THE TOP OF THE CAKE (OPTIONAL)

Reserve a few tbsp of the batter

Unsweetened Cocoa Powder (sieved) = 8 g / 1 tbsp

(Note: Mix together until well combined. The color should appear to be much darker than the batter. Fill into a piping bag and cut a small hole just before using.)

DIRECTIONS

1. Preheat the oven at 300F or 150C.

2. Prepare a pan. I used a 6 inch (15 cm) square pan with a removable bottom. Line the pan with parchment papers. The parchment paper for the side of the pan should be taller than the pan.

3. Sieve the coconut flour and unsweetened cocoa powder together into a bowl. Mix to combine.

4. Add the coconut oil, milk, vanilla extract and whisk to combine.

5. Add the 5 egg yolks and whisk until well combined. Set aside.

6. In another bowl, add the 5 egg whites, salt and beat with a handheld mixer at medium speed. Gradually add the sweetener while beating the egg whites until soft peaks. Soft peaks means that the tip of the peak will curve or fold back on itself.

7. Add 1/3 of the meringue into the chocolate mixture and fold to combine. This meringue is very important so try not to break it by mixing or stirring as the air will be deflated resulting in the cake unable to rise. Instead, fold gently as in scooping up so as to maintain its gentle shape. Also, do not over fold.

8. Pour the chocolate mixture into the meringue and fold to combine. The batter is silky-smooth.

9. Transfer the batter into the pan. Remember to reserve a few tbsp if you are opting to make the leaf design at the top of the cake.

10. Tap the pan a few times to release air bubbles.

11. Use the filled piping bag to create lines on the top of the cake. Then use a wooden skewer or toothpick to make the leaf design.

12. Fill hot water (not boiling water) into a suitable bigger pan. Make sure the water is sufficient so that you do not need to open the oven door to refill as this may affect the baking process.

13. Place an empty pan over the water and place the pan with batter on the empty pan. I used an extra pan as my pan has a removable bottom. If your pan has a solid base, then you don't need the extra pan. Just place the pan with batter directly on the pan with water.

Directions

14. Bake at the lowest rack for 50 to 60 mins.
15. The cake is done when it feels firm at the top.
16. After baking, immediately remove the cake from the pan and release the sides of the parchment paper and let it cool. Be careful when removing the sides of the parchment paper as they may stick to the cake and since the cake is delicate, gently use a spatula to help with the release. Unlike the Japanese Cheesecake, this castella cake does not deflate but if it does, it will be just a tiny bit.
17. Every oven is different so you may need to watch the heat and adjust accordingly.
18. This cake can be cut into 6 or 9 servings.
19. This cake can be enjoyed warm or chilled.

Total Servings = 9

Nutrition info per serving (Coconut flour version)
Total Carb = 2.1 g Dietary Fiber = 1.1 g Net Carb = 1.0 g
Calories = 89 g Total Fat = 8.1 g Protein = 3.7 g

Nutrition info per serving (Almond flour version)
Total Carb = 3.7 g Dietary Fiber = 1.9 g Net Carb = 1.8 g
Calories = 140 g Total Fat = 12.3 g Protein = 5.6 g

Tiramisu Cheesecake

DRY INGREDIENTS

Coconut flour = 90 g / 3/4 cup

(OR Almond flour = 360 g / 3 cups)

(OR Almond flour = 180 g / 1 1/2 cups + Coconut flour = 45 g / 5 3/4 tbsp)

Baking powder = 12 g / 3 tsp

Baking soda = 4 g / 1 tsp (optional)

Salt = 4 g / 1 tsp

Monk fruit = 120 g / 5/8 cup

Cocoa powder (unsweetened) = 35 g / 1/3 cup

Espresso powder = 4 g / 1 tsp (optional)

WET INGREDIENTS

Whole Eggs = 6 large (345 g)

Whipping cream = 315 ml / 1 1/3 cups

Unsalted Melted butter = 100 ml / 1/2 cup

Instant Coffee powder = 15 g / 3 tbsp. (Dissolve with 15 ml / 1 tbsp. hot water)

Some cocoa powder (unsweetened) for dusting

INGREDIENTS FOR CREAM CHEESE FROSTING

Cream cheese = 375 g / 1 1/2 bricks

Powdered sweetener = 176 g / 0.9 cup

Instant Coffee powder = 13 g / 2 1/2 tbsp. (dissolved with 15 ml / 1 tbsp. hot water)

Whipping cream = 160 ml / 2/3 cup

DIRECTIONS FOR THE CAKE

1. Preheat the oven at 340F or 170C.
2. In a big bowl, mix all the dry ingredients with a spatula until well combined.
3. Add all the wet ingredients and whisk until well combined. The batter is thick and smooth.
4. Transfer batter into a 12 inch (30 cm) square pan lined with parchment paper and spread evenly. You can also use rectangle or round baking pans or even paper cups.
5. Bake at the lowest rack for about 15 to 20 minutes or until a wooden skewer comes out clean. This cake cooks pretty quickly so do not over bake it.
6. Cool the cake completely.

DIRECTIONS FOR THE CREAM

1. In a bowl, add the cream cheese, powdered sweetener and use a handheld mixer to beat until smooth and creamy.
2. Add the whipping cream, coffee mixture and beat until well combined.
3. Chill until ready to use.

DIRECTIONS FOR ASSEMBLING THE CAKE

1. Cut the cake into half. As an option, you can trim the sides of the cake a little.
2. Spread half the cream onto the bottom layer of the cake.
3. Stack with the other half of the cake then top with the balance of the cream. Spread evenly.
4. Dust the top of cake with unsweetened cocoa powder.
5. Chill the cake for about 1 hour to set the cream a bit.
6. Cut into 18 servings.

Total Servings = 18

Nutrition info per serving (Coconut flour version)
Total Carb = 2.9 g Dietary Fiber = 0.9 g Net Carb = 2.0 g
Calories = 219 g Total Fat = 21.9 g Protein = 4.5 g

Nutrition info per serving (Almond flour version)
Total Carb = 5.4 g Dietary Fiber = 2.1 g Net Carb = 3.3 g
Calories = 296 g Total Fat = 28.1 g Protein = 7.3 g

Nutrition info per serving (Almond & Coconut flour version)
Total Carb = 4.1 g Dietary Fiber = 1.5 g Net Carb = 2.6 g
Calories = 258 g Total Fat = 25.0 g Protein = 5.9 g

Tuna Muffins

DRY INGREDIENTS

Almond flour = 120 g / 1 cup

Coconut four = 30 g / 1/4 cup

Other flour options :

1. Almond flour = 240 g / 2 cups

2. Coconut flour = 60 g / 1/2 cup (The amount of pea or almond milk should be 120 ml / 1/2 cup. All other ingredients remains the same)

Monk fruit = 30 g / 2 1/3 tbsp (This adds just a hint of sweetness but it's optional)

Baking Powder = 10 g / 2 1/2 tsp

Salt = 1/2 tsp

WET INGREDIENTS

Whole Eggs = 4 large (230 g)

Unsalted Melted Butter = 60 ml / 1/4 cup

Unsweetened Pea or Almond Milk = 60 ml / 1/4 cup

INGREDIENTS FOR TUNA FILLINGS

Canned tuna = 110 g net / 1 can (liquid or oil drained off)

Frozen carrots & peas = 50 g / 1/2 cup

Keto friendly mayonnaise = 90 g / 6/14 tbsp

Sour cream = 30 g / 2 tbsp

Salt = 1/2 tsp

Black pepper = 1/4 tsp

Chopped parsley for garnishing

DIRECTIONS

1. Preheat the oven at 340F or 170C.
2. In a bowl, add all the dry ingredients and mix until well combined.
3. Add all the wet ingredients and whisk until well combined. The batter is thick and smooth. Set aside.
4. In a separate bowl, mash the tuna until a finer texture. Add the rest of the ingredients and mix until well combined. Adjust taste accordingly. Set aside.
5. Spoon the batter into the muffin mold until half full. I used a silicone muffin mold (lightly greased) and it yielded 11 tuna muffins. I like to use silicone molds as they make removal of the muffins super easy.
6. Spoon the tuna fillings over the batter.
7. Bake at the middle rack for 20 to 25 minutes or until a wooden skewer comes out clean. However, please ensure that you prick the wooden skewer into the muffin area, not the filling for accuracy.
8. Cool for a bit as these tuna muffins taste great when still warm.

Total Servings = 11

Nutrition info per serving
Total Carb = 2.7 g Dietary Fiber = 1.2 g Net Carb = 1.5 g
Calories = 187 g Total Fat = 16.8 g Protein = 6.4 g

Vanilla & Chocolate Mug Cakes

INGREDIENTS FOR VANILLA CAKE

Dry Ingredients

	Coconut Flour	Almond Flour
Flour amount	3 tbsp	6 tbsp
Baking Powder	1/2 tsp	1/2 tsp
Monk fruit	3 to 4 tbsp	3 to 4 tbsp
Salt	A pinch	A pinch

Wet Ingredients

	Coconut Flour	Almond Flour
Whole egg	1 large	1 large
Unsweetened Pea or Almond Milk	3 tbsp	1 tbsp
Coconut Oil (Or butter / olive oil)	2 tbsp	1 tbsp
Vanilla Extract	1/2 tsp	1/2 tsp

INGREDIENTS FOR CHOCOLATE CAKE

Dry Ingredients

	Coconut Flour	Almond Flour
Flour amount	2 tbsp	5 tbsp
Unsweetened Cocoa Powder	2 tsp	2 tsp
Baking Powder	1/2 tsp	1/2 tsp
Monk fruit	3 to 4 tbsp	3 to 4 tbsp
Salt	A pinch	A pinch

Wet Ingredients	Coconut Flour	Almond Flour
Whole egg	1 large	1 large
Unsweetened Pea or Almond Milk	3 tbsp	1 tbsp
Coconut Oil	2 tbsp	1 tbsp
Vanilla Extract (optional)	1/2 tsp	1/2 tsp

DIRECTIONS

1. Single serving cakes are the only exception that I will not be weighing the ingredients as they are so small in amount. However, it's important that you use the same set of measuring spoons for accuracy.

2. Add all the dry ingredients into a cup, mug or ramekin. I used a 200ml cup so please adjust the recipe according to the size of cup, mug or ramekin that you are using. Mix the ingredients until well combined.

3. Add all the wet ingredients and mix until smooth.

4. Microwave at high for 1 to 2 mins. Try at 1 min first and if it is not cooked yet, just microwave at 30 second intervals.

5. Remove from microwave, decorate with little fresh strawberries or blueberries and dust with powdered sweetener (optional).

6. If you opt to add the unsweetened peanut butter to the chocolate cake, just use a knife to cut a small hole in the middle of the cake and remove the cake with a spoon. Fill the hole with peanut butter then top with the cut cake.

Total Servings = 1

Nutrition info per serving (Vanilla Coconut Flour Version) Total
Carb = 2.4 g Dietary Fiber = 1.2 g Net Carb = 1.2 g Calories = 297 g
Total Fat = 30.3 g Protein = 6.2 g

Nutrition info per serving (Vanilla Almond Flour Version)
Total Carb = 5.6 g Dietary Fiber = 2.6 g Net Carb = 3.0 g
Calories = 320 g Total Fat = 28.9 g Protein = 10.7 g

Nutrition info per serving (Chocolate Coconut Flour Version)
Total Carb = 4.6 g Dietary Fiber = 2.6 g Net Carb = 2.0 g
Calories = 304 g Total Fat = 30.8 g Protein = 7.0 g

Nutrition info per serving (Chocolate Almond Flour Version)
Total Carb = 7.5 g Dietary Fiber = 3.9 g Net Carb = 3.6 g
Calories = 308 g Total Fat = 27.7 g Protein = 10.9 g

Vanilla Cake With Buttercream

DRY INGREDIENTS

Coconut flour = 120 g / 1 cup

(OR Almond flour = 480 g / 4 cups

Baking Powder = 14 g / 1 tbsp

Monk fruit = 50 g / 1/4 cup (Note: This small amount is to balance out the sweetness from the frosting. If you are not doing frosting, you need to increase the sweetener to 120 to 150 g.)

Salt = 4 g / 1 tsp

WET INGREDIENTS

Whipping Cream = 320 ml / 1.3 cups

Whole Eggs = 6 large (345 g)

Melted Unsalted Butter = 120 ml / 1/2 cup

Vanilla Extract = 13 g / 1 tbsp (Note: You can add more for a stronger flavor)

INGREDIENTS FOR VANILLA BUTTERCREAM FROSTING

Unsalted Butter (room temperature) = 450 g / 2 cups

Powdered Sweetener = 200 g / 1 1/2 cups

Whipping Cream = 120 ml / 1/2 cup

Salt = 4 g / 1 tsp

Vanilla Extract = 13 g / 1 tbsp (Note: You may add more for a stronger flavor)

DIRECTIONS FOR THE CAKE

1. Preheat the oven at 340 F or 170 C.
2. In a bowl, add all the wet ingredients and whisk until well combined. Set aside.
3. In another bowl, add all the dry ingredients and mix until well combined.
4. Add the wet into the dry ingredients and whisk until the batter is smooth and thick.
5. Transfer the batter into 2 x 8 or 9 inch (20 or 23 cm) greased pans lined with parchment paper at the bottom. Weigh and divide the batter equally.
6. Bake at the middle rack for 20 mins or until a wooden skewer comes out clean.
7. Cool the cakes for 10 minutes before removing from pan.
8. Remove the cakes from the pans and let them cool completely upside down on a wire rack.
9. Meanwhile, prepare the vanilla buttercream.

DIRECTIONS FOR THE VANILLA BUTTERCREAM

1. Beat the butter until light and fluffy.
2. Then add the powdered sweetener and beat to combine.
3. Add the whipping cream, salt, vanilla extract and beat until well combined.

DIRECTIONS FOR ASSEMBLING & FROSTING THE CAKE

1. Place one layer of the cake on a cake tray upside down.
2. Spoon some buttercream onto the top of the cake and spread evenly.
3. Top with the second layer of cake. Make sure both cakes are even to prevent a lopsided cake.
4. Spread some buttercream evenly on the top and sides of the cake. The frosting does not have to look perfect but because we are creating waves with the frosting, we need to have thicker layer of the frosting.
5. Use the back of a spoon to create waves at the sides and top of the cake
6. Decorate with whole strawberries or sugar free sprinkles
7. Chill the cake for 30 to 60 minutes before slicing.

Total Servings = 12

Nutrition info per serving (Coconut flour version)
Total Carb = 2.3 g Dietary Fiber = 0.5 g Net Carb = 1.8 g
Calories = 186 g Total Fat = 18.5 g Protein = 3.6 g

Nutrition info per serving (Almond flour version)
Total Carb = 7.2 g Dietary Fiber = 2.9 g Net Carb = 4.3 g
Calories = 340 g Total Fat = 31.0 g Protein = 9.2 g

Nutrition info per serving (Buttercream)
Total Carb = 0.3 g Dietary Fiber = 0 g Net Carb = 0.3 g
Calories = 298 g Total Fat = 33.6 g Protein = 0.5 g

Vanilla Sponge Cake

INGREDIENTS FOR CAKE

Coconut flour = 30 g / 1/4 cup

(OR Almond Flour = 90 g / 3/4 cup)

Whole Eggs = 3 large (170 g)

Monk fruit = 50 g / 1/4 cup

Coconut or olive oil = 30 ml / 2 tbsp.

White vinegar = 1 tsp (this helps to remove the eggy taste)

Vanilla extract = 1 to 2 tsp

Garnishing = Handful of strawberries and blueberries (optional)

INGREDIENTS FOR WHIPPED CREAM ICING

Heavy or whipping cream = 360 g / 1 1/2 cups

Powdered sweetener = 30 g / 4 tbsp.

Lemon juice = 1/2 to 1 lemon

Lemon zest = 1 lemon

[Note = Beat cream until fluffy then add powdered sweetener, lemon juice, zest and beat for a little while more. Refrigerate if not using immediately.]

DIRECTIONS

1. Preheat the oven at 320F or 160C.

2. Prepare a 6 inch or 15 cm spring form pan or solid base pan. Line with parchment paper at the bottom of pan. It's not necessary to grease the sides of pan or line with parchment paper as this will provide a better grip for the cake to rise.

3. In a bowl, beat the eggs, sweetener, vinegar and vanilla extract with a handheld or stand mixer at medium speed for about 5 to 6 mins or until it reaches a ribbon consistency i.e. you can draw lines with the batter. The volume will be tripled. Do not over beat the eggs until stiff peaks as this will cause the cake to collapse during baking.

4. Add the coconut flour gradually and fold gently until combined. The folding process is like scooping up something gently. Do not stir or mix as this will deflate the batter.

5. In a separate small bowl, add a little bit of the batter to the coconut oil and mix until well combined. Then add back into the batter and fold until combined.

6. Transfer the batter into the pan. Gently shake the sides a little and tap the pan a few times to remove air bubbles.

7. Bake for about 30 mins or until a skewer comes out clean.

8. Cool for 15 mins then remove cake and paper from the pan.

9. If using whipped cream icing, spread on top of cake and top with berries of your choice.

Total Servings = 8

Nutrition info per serving
Total Car'b = 1.8 g Dietary Fiber = 0.2 g Net Carb = 1.6 g
Calories = 187 g Total Fat = 19.1 g Protein = 3.1 g

Walnut Cake With Buttercream

DRY INGREDIENTS

Raw Walnuts = 240 g / 2 cups

Coconut Flour = 60 g / 1/2 cup

Baking Powder = 12 g / 3 tsp

Baking Soda = 1/2 tsp (Optional)

Salt = 1 tsp

Monk fruit = 50 g / 1/4 cup (This is a reduced amount to balance the sweetness level from the frosting. If you are not doing the frosting then you need to increase the sweetener amount to about 100 to 120 g)

Chopped Walnuts = 30 g / 1/4 cup (Optional)

WET INGREDIENTS

Whole Eggs = 5 large (290 g)

Unsalted Melted Butter = 60 ml / 1/4 cup

Whipping Cream = 240 ml / 1 cup

Vanilla Extract = 2 tsp

INGREDIENTS FOR BUTTERCREAM

Unsalted Butter (room temperature) = 120 g / 1/2 cup

Powdered sweetener = 90 g / 3/4 cup

Whipping or heavy cream = 2 tbsp.

Salt = 1 tsp

Vanilla extract = 2 tsp

Lemon juice = 2 tbsp (Optional)

Garnishing = 1 whole strawberry for each square of cake or to reduce carb content, you could top with sliced strawberries.

DIRECTIONS FOR THE CAKE

1. Preheat the oven at 350F or 180C.
2. Grind the raw walnuts together with the coconut flour in a multi grinder until a finer texture. It is fine if there are still some chunks. Home grinding will not produce a super fine texture as the fat content of the nuts are still intact. Hence, the coconut flour helps to absorb the excess fats and ease with the grinding process. Do not over grind as it will turn into a paste of butter.
3. In a bowl, mix all the dry ingredients.
4. Add all the wet ingredients and whisk until smooth and thick.
5. Transfer batter into a 7 inch (18 cm) square pan lined with parchment paper.
6. Bake for about 40 minutes or until a wooden skewer comes out clean.
7. Cool completely.
8. Frost the top of the cake with the buttercream, garnish with fresh strawberries then cut into 25x1 inch squares.

DIRECTIONS FOR THE BUTTERCREAM FROSTING

1. In a bowl, beat the butter with a handheld mixer until the color turns lighter.
2. Add the powdered sweetener and beat until well combined, smooth and creamy.
3. Add the whipping cream, salt, vanilla extract, lemon juice (if using) and beat until

well combined and smooth.

Total Servings = 25

Nutrition info per serving
Total Carb = 1.7 g Dietary Fiber = 0.8 g Net Carb = 0.9 g
Calories = 119 g Total Fat = 11.5 g Protein = 3.7 g

Walnut Carrot Cake With Cream Cheese Frosting

DRY INGREDIENTS FOR THE CAKE

Raw Walnuts = 240 g / 2 cups

Coconut flour = 60 g / 1/2 cup

Baking Powder = 12 g / 3 tsp

Salt = 4 g / 1 tsp

Monk fruit = 100 g / 1/2 cup

Ground Cinnamon = 11 g / 4 tsp (Note: You can use between 2 to 4 tsp according to your preference)

All Spice = 12 g / 3 tsp

Grated carrots = 115 g / 1 cup

Chopped walnuts = 60 g / 1/2 cup

WET INGREDIENTS FOR THE CAKE

Whole Eggs = 5 large (290 g)

Unsalted Melted Butter = 60 ml / 1/4 cup

Whipping Cream = 240 ml / 1 cup

INGREDIENTS FOR CREAM CHEESE FROSTING

Cream Cheese (softened) = 350 g / 1 1/2 cup

Zest = 1 lemon (optional)

Powdered Sweetener = 100 g / 1/2 cup

DIRECTIONS FOR THE CAKE

1. Preheat the oven at 350F or 180C.

2. Grind the raw walnuts together with the coconut flour in a multi grinder until a finer texture. It is fine if there are still some chunks. Home grinding will not produce a super fine texture as the fat content of the nuts are still intact. Hence, the coconut flour helps to absorb the excess fats and ease with the grinding process. Do not over grind as it will turn into a paste of butter.

3. In a bowl, mix all the dry ingredients until well combined. For the grated carrots, add half only and reserve the the other half for the toppings.

4. Add all the wet ingredients and whisk until well combined, smooth and thick.

5. Transfer batter equally into 2 x 8 inch (20 cm) round shallow pans that are greased and lined with parchment paper.

6. Bake for 30 mins or until a wooden skewer comes out clean. Let it cool completely on a wire rack.

7. Apply half the cream cheese frosting on the bottom layer of the cake and spread evenly. Top with half the reserved grated carrots.

8. Top with second layer of cake.

9. Apply the balance of cream cheese frosting on the top layer of cake and spread evenly. Dust with ground cinnamon and top with the balance of grated carrots.

DIRECTIONS FOR THE CREAM CHEESE FROSTING

1. Using a handheld or stand mixer, beat the cream cheese and sweetener until light and fluffy.

2. Then add the lemon zest (if using) and mix to combine. Set aside. You can chill it in the fridge if not using immediately.

Total Servings = 12

Nutrition info per serving
Total Car'b = 6.5 g Dietary Fiber = 3.4 g Net Carb = 3.1 g
Calories = 408 g Total Fat = 39.1 g Protein = 9.4 g

Walnut Chocolate Cake

DRY INGREDIENTS

Raw Walnuts = 240 g / 2 cups

Coconut Flour = 60 g / 1/2 cup

Baking Powder = 12 g / 3 tsp

Unsweetened Cocoa Powder = 30 g / 4

tbsp Monk fruit = 100g / 1/2 cup

Salt = 2 g / 1/2 tsp

WET INGREDIENTS

Whole Eggs = 5 large (290 g)

Unsalted Melted Butter = 60 ml / 1/4

cup Whipping Cream = 240 ml / 1 cup

Vanilla Extract = 2 tsp

INGREDIENTS FOR CHOCOLATE GANACHE

Unsweetened dark chocolate = 113 g / 4 oz

Whipping or heavy cream = 120 ml / 1/2 cup

Monk fruit = 70 g / 1/3 cup

DIRECTIONS FOR THE CAKE

1. Preheat the oven at 340F or 170C

2. Grind the raw walnuts together with the coconut flour in a multi grinder until a finer texture. It is fine if there are still some chunks. Home grinding will not produce a super fine texture as the fat content of the nuts are still intact. Hence, the coconut flour helps to absorb the excess fats and ease with the grinding process. Do not over grind as it will turn into a paste of butter.

3. In a bowl, add all the wet ingredients and whisk until well combined. Set aside.

4. In another bowl, add all the dry ingredients and mix until well combined. Remember to sieve the cocoa powder to prevent any clumps.

5. Add the wet into the dry ingredients and whisk until well combined. The batter is thick and smooth.

6. Transfer batter into a greased pan lined with parchment paper at the bottom. I used a 7 1/2 inch (19 cm) pan with a removable bottom. You can also use an 8 inch (20 cm) pan or any suitable pan.

7. Shake and tap the pan gently to remove any air bubbles in the batter.

8. Bake at the middle rack for 40 to 50 minutes or until a wooden skewer comes out clean.

9. Cool the cake completely on a wire rack before frosting.

DIRECTIONS FOR THE CHOCOLATE GANACHE

1. Mix all ingredients in a bowl.

2. Melt the ingredients in the microwave at 30 seconds interval or you can melt over the stove with low heat.

3. Spread the chocolate ganache evenly on the top of the cake.

4. Decorate with whole strawberries

5. Sprinkle with flaky sea salt.

6. Chill the cake for 30 minutes before slicing.

Total Servings = 12

Nutrition info per serving (For the Cake)
Total Carb = 4.8 g Dietary Fiber = 2.5 g Net Carb = 2.3 g
Calories = 208 g Total Fat = 20.0 g Protein = 5.8 g

Nutrition info per serving (For the Chocolate Ganache)
Total Carb = 3.2 g Dietary Fiber = 1.3 g Net Carb = 1.9 g
Calories = 93 g Total Fat = 8.0 g Protein = 1.3 g

Walnut Coffee Cake

DRY INGREDIENTS

Raw Walnuts = 120 g / 1 cup

Coconut Flour = 40 g / 1/3 cup

Baking Powder = 8 g / 1/2 tsp

Monk fruit = 80 g / 6 1/2 tbsp

Salt = 2 g / 1/2 tsp

WET INGREDIENTS

Whole Eggs = 3 large (170 g)

Unsalted Melted Butter = 60 ml / 1/4

cup Whipping Cream = 180 ml / 3/4 cup

Instant Coffee Powder = 20 g (4 tbsp) (If you prefer a stronger coffee flavor, you can add more coffee powder but you may need to increase the sweetener otherwise, it will be quite bitter. Alternatively, you can add coffee extract for a stronger flavor)

Hot water = 30 ml / 2 tbsp

DIRECTIONS

1. Preheat the oven at 340F or 170C

2. Grind the raw walnuts together with the coconut flour in a multi grinder until a finer texture. It is fine if there are still some chunks. Home grinding will not produce a super fine texture as the fat content of the nuts are still intact. Hence, the coconut flour helps to absorb the excess fats and ease with the grinding process. Do not over grind as it will turn into a paste of butter.

3. Dissolve the instant coffee powder with the hot water and set aside.

4. In a bowl, add all the dry ingredients and mix until well combined.

5. Add all the wet ingredients and whisk until well combined.

6. Add the dissolved coffee powder and whisk until the batter is thick and smooth.

7. Transfer batter into a greased pan lined with parchment paper at the bottom. I used a 6 inch (15 cm) pan with a removable bottom. You can also use any suitable pan.

8. Tap the pan gently a few times then top with walnuts (optional)

9. Bake at the middle rack for 40 to 50 minutes or until a wooden skewer comes out clean. As this cake is thicker than my other 6 inch pan cake recipes, you may want to bake slightly longer to ensure that the center of the cake is cooked.

10. Cool the cake then dust with powdered sweetener (optional)

Total Servings = 8

Nutrition info per serving
Total Carb = 3.2 g Dietary Fiber = 1.3 g Net Carb = 1.9 g
Calories `= 241 g Total Fat = 23.7 g Protein = 6.4 g

Yogurt Lemon Cake

DRY INGREDIENTS

Coconut flour = 60 g / 1/2 cup

(OR Almond flour = 240 g / 2 cups)

Baking Powder = 8 g / 2 tsp

Monk fruit = 50 g / 1/4 cup

Zest from 1 lemon

A pinch of salt

WET INGREDIENTS

Unsweetened Greek or Plain Yogurt = 160 g / 2/3 cup

Whole Eggs = 3 large (170 g)

Coconut Oil = 60 ml / 1/4 cup

Fresh lemon juice = 15 ml / 1 tbsp (If you prefer a stronger lemon taste, you can add up to 30 ml or 2 tbsp)

Vanilla extract = 1 tsp

DIRECTIONS

1. Preheat the oven at 340 F or 170 C.
2. In a bowl, add all the wet ingredients and whisk until well combined. Set aside.
3. In another bowl, add all the dry ingredients and mix until well combined.
4. Add the wet into the dry ingredients and whisk until well combined. The batter is thick and smooth.
5. Transfer the batter in a greased pan lined with parchment paper at the bottom. I used a 6 inch or 15 cm round pan with a removable bottom. You can also use a spring form pan. Spread evenly.
6. Bake at the middle rack for 30 to 35 mins or until cooked.
7. Cool completely.
8. Dust with powdered sweetener (optional).

Total Servings = 8

Nutrition info per serving (Coconut flour version)
Total Carb = 1.6 g Dietary Fiber = 0.4 g Net Carb = 1.2 g
Calories = 104 g Total Fat = 9.1 g Protein = 4.3 g
`
Nutrition info per serving (Almond flour version)
Total Carb = 5.3 g Dietary Fiber = 2.1 g Net Carb = 3.2 g
Calories = 220 g Total Fat = 18.4 g Protein = 8.4 g

Zebra Cake

DRY INGREDIENTS

Coconut Flour = 90 g / 3/4 cup

(OR Almond Flour = 360 g / 3 cups)

Baking Powder = 12 g / 3 tsp

Baking Soda = 1/2 tsp

Monk fruit = 120 g / 0.6 cup

Unsweetened Cocoa Powder = 25 g / 3

tbsp Salt = 1/2 tsp

WET INGREDIENTS

Whole Eggs = 4 large (230 g)

Melted Unsalted Butter = 60 ml / 1/4

cup Whipping Cream = 240 ml / 1 cup

Vanilla Extract = 3 tsp

Water = 60 ml / 1/4 cup

DIRECTIONS

1. Preheat oven at 340F or 170C.

2. In a bowl, mix all the dry ingredients (except the cocoa powder) until well combined. Set aside.

3. In a separate bowl, mix all the wet ingredients (except the water) until well combined.

4. Add the wet ingredients into the dry ingredients and mix until smooth and thick.

5. Divide the batter into 2 equal portions.

6. Add the unsweetened cocoa powder and water into one of the batters and mix until well combined.

7. Grease and line parchment paper at the bottom of an 8" or 20 cm round pan.

8. Spoon the batter onto the middle of the pan, alternating between the original and chocolate batter until all the batter is used up.

9. The batter will spread naturally.

10. Tap the pan for a few times.

11. Bake for about 30 to 40 mins or until a wooden skewer comes out clean.

Total Servings = 12

Nutrition info per serving (Coconut flour version)
Total Carb = 2.5 g Dietary Fiber = 1.1 g Net Carb = 1.4 g
Calories = 83 g Total Fat = 7.2 g Protein = 2.7 g

Nutrition info per serving (Almond flour version)
Total Carb = 6.2 g Dietary Fiber = 2.9 g Net Carb = 3.3 g
Calories = 198 g Total Fat = 16.5 g Protein = 6.8 g

Thank you for your support! If you find this e-book useful, do check out my other books on low carb / keto recipes.

I publish two new videos per week on Mondays and Thursdays in my youtube channel so do subscribe to my youtube channel at "lowcarbrecipeideas".

I would love to see your pictures when you make any of my recipes so feel free to tag me at Facebook, Instagram or just email to me at "lowcarbrecipeideas@gmail.com". I repost most of these pictures in my social medias to share with everyone.

If you have any reviews, enquiries or suggestions, feel free to drop me an email. Once again, thank you for your support!

 Https://youtube.com/lowcarbrecipeideas

 Https://facebook.com/lowcarbrecipeidea

 Https://instagram.com/lowcarbrecipeideas

Printed in Great Britain
by Amazon

43506544R00110